The Series

A Photographic Look at the Inaugural Bassmaster ELITE SERIES
by Doug Cox & Steve Bowman

DEDICATION

This book is dedicated to the 106 anglers who competed in the inaugural season of the CITGO Bassmaster Elite Series. Their dedication, passion and skill changed the bass-fishing landscape forever.

FOREWORD

by Tommy Sanders

I have covered the sport of professional bass fishing for ten years on television, or for about one quarter of its 40-year history. It's a young sport, to be sure, sixty years or more behind baseball, golf and tennis. As for all the talk of the great traditions, the past glories and "the way we used to do it," the truth is it's a sport only in its adolescence. The game as it's played is still evolving. The body of knowledge is expanding rapidly, and the techniques and equipment get more sophisticated with each passing year.

The year 2006 will stand as the year professional bass fishing turned a major corner. The changes were these: a smaller, more elite field for the tournament series at the highest level with more than 100 pros; a new name - The CITGO Bassmaster Elite Series - naturally; more tournaments - the previous season, Bassmaster pros fished only six regular season tour events, but in 2006, they would fish eleven, February through September; Majors - for the top fifty or so qualifiers, three new all-star events were added to the schedule, with a quarter of a million dollars to each winner.

The real meaning of this was each of these Elite Series anglers was asked to become, more than ever before, a full-time, big-time professional. That would mean major commitments in time, major financial commitments, and most importantly, a commitment to go out and prove you could compete, for the better part of a year, with the best in the world.

It was a lot to ask, but the anglers gave us more than we could have ever hoped for. It's a season that started with a Classic on Lake Toho, a site where records have been set in the past and where a major Classic record was set again this year. Then the regular season commenced at a true bass fishing wonderland, Lake Amistad, where you could see giant largemouth swimming through submerged treetops in 30 feet of crystal clear water. Not to mention the excitement of watching Ish Monroe find the biggest fish and somehow find a way to put them in the boat. Then another Texas stop at a perennial favorite, Sam Rayburn Reservoir, where Greg Hackney put to rest any doubts about his ability to win big ones, taking his second top level Bassmaster win.

The trail headed through the southeast, to Santee Cooper, where another record was set - 115 lbs and 15 ounces for four days of fishing by Preston Clark. Next was legendary Lake Guntersville in Alabama, where a packed house told winner Mike Iaconelli that celebrating a big win in the most extreme manner possible is just what the people want to see. Then there was Clarks Hill in Georgia, where Davy Hite showed us that home water knowledge and a love for fishing in the month of May are a powerful combination.

Two tournament stops, at Grand Lake in Oklahoma and Kentucky Lake, brought the pros back to some water they hadn't seen for a while. Mike McClelland did his homework better than anyone else and won at Grand, and Morizo Shimizu became the second Japanese angler to win a top level event at Kentucky Lake. After that, the Northern Swing brought the Elite Series to a pair of famous smallmouth fisheries, New York's Oneida Lake and Lake Champlain, only to see a couple of wily largemouth fishing veterans seize the day - Tommy Biffle at Oneida and Denny Brauer at Champlain. There were fireworks for Kelly Jordon on the

THE HOSTS - Tommy Sanders (right) and Mark Zona (left) are the hosts of the "The Bassmasters" television show. The duo highlighted the victories and heartbreaks of the Elite Series on ESPN2.

Potomac River in Maryland and a bang up finish by Todd Faircloth and the crowning of Mike Iaconelli as the 2006 Angler of the Year at Missouri's Table Rock Lake.

Then there were the Majors, which saw another veteran take the first quarter of a million dollar prize of the year at Lake Benbrook and Eagle Mountain Lake in Ft. Worth, and two first time Bassmaster winners at North Carolina's Lake Wylie and on the Arkansas River in Little Rock.

Words don't really do justice to the amazing things we saw on the water during this unforgettable year. But on these pages, you'll see the magic moments that tell the story in an unforgettable way. It's a tribute to the greatest anglers in this unique sport, who took their game to a place it has never been before.

ACKNOWLEDGMENT

This book would not have been possible without the enormous support and help from a long list of people.

At the top of that list is Don Rucks, whose vision for the sport not only created the Elite Series, but also commissioned this project. Rucks is the former General Manager of BASS. This is part of his legacy.

Along with him are Dave Precht and Amy Skiff, who nurtured this project through to fruition. And the entire Bassmaster tournament crew who put up with Doug Cox and Steve Bowman sticking their lenses every place they could.

The same could be said for JM Associates, the company that produces the Bassmaster Television show on ESPN2. Besides employing Bowman, they helped create the book in more ways than can be listed.

James Overstreet deserves a ton of credit. Some of his images appear in this book. Without Overstreet, it would have been difficult to fill in the blanks.

There is also Gerald Crawford, the dean of Bassmaster photographers. He's paved the way for every Bassmaster photographer and continues to show us up with great images.

The creative powerhouse behind this project was an extremely talented team of designers: Bill Zwerger, Sarah Paulin and Cherrill Cohen of the Cox Group and Michael Puckett of the Puckett Studio. Thank you for all your hard work, last-minute changes and working late just one more time.

And last, but certainly not least, the 106 professional anglers who laid everything on the line, competed on a level never before seen and created so many unforgettable scenes, some of which are in this book.

To all the above and so many more, thank you.

BASS logo, Bassmaster ELITE SERIES, Bassmaster Memorial, Bassmaster American, Bassmaster Legends and Bassmaster Angler of the Year are trademarks of BASS LLC.

ISBN-13: 987-0-9786952-1-7
ISBN-10: 0-9786952-1-6

All rights reserved. No part of this book may be reproduced or transmitted in any form or by any electronic or mechanical means, including photocopying, recording or by any information storage and retrieval system, without written permission from the publisher, except for the inclusion of brief quotations in a review.

Copyright © 2006 by Doug Cox and Steve Bowman

CONTENTS

CHAPTER 1 – Bassmaster Classic   6
The first early spring Bassmaster Classic lived up to its billing with record stringers and big bass. Luke Clausen set a record for the heaviest winning total.

CHAPTER 2 – Battle on the Border   16
Lake Amistad surprised everyone, with its big bass and huge stringers. But it was the perfect destination to start the Elite Series and for Ish Monroe to win his first event.

CHAPTER 3 – Lone Star Shootout   24
Sam Rayburn was back to reality for the Elite Series anglers, and Greg Hackney proved why he is quickly becoming one of the best ever.

CHAPTER 4 – Santee Cooper Showdown   32
All the records were supposed to be broken by the time the Santee Cooper Showdown took place. But Preston Clark had other things on his mind.

CHAPTER 5 – Southern Challenge   44
Michael Iaconelli had an unbelievable year, one that included a last-second catch that gave him a win at Lake Guntersville and put him on his way to winning the sport's most-prized title.

CHAPTER 6 – Pride of Augusta   52
Davy Hite used a big, moppy-like jig and an intimate knowledge of the habits of the blueback herring on Clark's Hill to win one for the family.

CHAPTER 7 – Bassmaster Memorial   60
The Bassmaster Memorial was a tribute to Don Butler, but it was a heyday for Peter Thliveros, who put together a big-fish strategy to win the first Major and the $250,000.

CHAPTER 8 – Sooner Run   74
Grand Lake was truly grand for Mike McClelland, after he jumped out to a big lead on Day One and just kept adding to the weight at the Sooner Run.

CHAPTER 9 – Bluegrass Brawl   82
Japanese angler Morizo Shimizu surprised the field by putting together one of the sport's best comebacks to win the Bluegrass Brawl.

CHAPTER 10 – Empire Chase   90
If Tommy Biffle had listened to conventional wisdom, he would have never figured into the Empire Chase. But he stayed with the largemouth and won.

CHAPTER 11 – Champion's Choice   98
Old dogs know all the tricks and Denny Brauer showed that he's still got a few tricks left to teach. He won the Champion's Choice by fishing a flawless event.

CHAPTER 12 – Bassmaster American   106
Jason Quinn was supposed to win the Bassmaster American, but Dave Wolak had other ideas. He won the event and the $250,000 just days after his first child was born.

CHAPTER 13 – Capitol Clash   118
Kelly Jordon is a master of catching big bass. On the Potomac River he figured out how to catch them to win the Capitol Clash.

CHAPTER 14 – Bassmaster Legends   126
The home-water jinx has a long and storied history in Bassmaster events. But Scott Rook withstood the jinx and a big charge by Shaw Grigsby to win the Bassmaster Legends.

CHAPTER 15 – The Rock   138
Finesse fishing isn't Todd Faircloth's forte, but after he won The Rock with a drop shot, he may become known for his ability to adapt.

Printed in the United States of America by RR Donnelley
Layout and design by Bill Zwerger, Sarah Paulin and Michael Puckett
Cover design by Cherrill Cohen (Cox Group)
Lake illustrations by Lenny McPherson

Published by: Bowman Outdoor Enterprises
3115 N. Rodney Parham
Little Rock, Ark. 72212
501-221-2282
www.theduckseason.com

Cox Group
149-B Rolling Hills Road
Mooresville, NC 28117
704-799-2114
www.coxgp.com

For more information visit
www.EliteSeriesBook.com
or call 704-799-2114

Bassmaster Classic
Lake Tohopekaliga

"It still really hasn't sunk in. I'm pretty much in disbelief. It's like I'm in the middle of a dream. When I was out there (on stage) and all that confetti is going on and I'm holding that trophy, it's surreal."
— *Luke Clausen*

KISSIMMEE, Fla. — It was all about the records in the 36th annual CITGO Bassmaster Classic on Lake Tohopekaliga. The lake that has produced more than its share of records in the past lived up to the high expectations of trophy bass and big catches.

On Day One the top four finishers broke the existing Bassmaster Classic record for the heaviest five-fish catch — 21 pounds, 8 ounces — set by Paul Elias on Lake Logan Martin in 1993. Luke Clausen led with 29 pounds, 6 ounces, Preston Clark was second with 29-1, Edwin Evers was third with 23-10 and Kevin Wirth was fourth with 22-5.

Clark also broke a record that had existed for 30 years. Ricky Green set the big-bass standard in the 1976 Classic on Lake Guntersville with an 8-pound, 9-ounce largemouth. But Clark's Purolator Big Bass on Day One weighed an impressive 11 pounds, 10 ounces.

Clausen, who led every day of the three-day event, set his own records too. His total 56 pounds, 2 ounces surpassed the previous Classic record Davy Hite set in 1999 of 55-10 on the Louisiana Delta.

"It still really hasn't sunk in," Clausen said. "I'm pretty much in disbelief. It's like I'm in the middle of a dream. When I was out there (on stage) and all that confetti is going on and I'm holding that trophy, it's surreal."

NOT-SO FAVORITE
Terry Scroggins was hailed as the odds-on favorite for the 2006 CITGO Bassmaster Classic on Lake Toho. But he had a slow start on Day One finishing in 37th place. His intimate knowledge of the lake, though, helped him rebound to a fourth place finish overall.

PASSING OF THE TROPHY - Kevin VanDam shakes Luke Clausen's hand after handing over the 2006 CITGO Bassmaster Classic trophy. Clausen led all three days of the event.

CLASSIC RECORDS

Largest "recorded" Big Bass in Classic history

1. Preston Clark — 11-10 — Day 1, 2006, Lake Toho
2. Rick Clunn — 10-10 — Day 1, 2006, Lake Toho
3. Mark Tucker — 9-10 — Day 1, 2006, Lake Toho
4. Terry Scroggins — 9-5 — Day 2, 2006, Lake Toho
5. Edwin Evers — 8-15 — Day 1, 2006, Lake Toho
6. Ricky Green — 8-9 — Day 2, 1976, Lake Guntersville
7. Ron Shuffield — 8-8 — Day 2, 2006, Lake Toho
8. Rick Clunn — 7-13 — Day 2, 1976, Lake Guntersville
9. Rick Clunn — 7-7 — Day 1, 1976, Lake Guntersville

Heaviest single-day 5-fish stringers caught in Classic history

1. Luke Clausen — 29-6 — Day 1, 2006, Lake Toho
2. Preston Clark — 29-1 — Day 1, 2006, Lake Toho
3. Terry Scroggins — 28-6 — Day 2, 2006, Lake Toho
4. Edwin Evers — 23-10 — Day 1, 2006, Lake Toho
5. Kevin Wirth — 22-5 — Day 1, 2006, Lake Toho
6. Paul Elias — 21-8 — 1993, Logan Martin

KNEELING AND REELING - Preston Clark, who finished sixth, stayed at the top of the standings by concentrating on spooky bedding fish. They were so spooky, Clark utilized a push pole to move around the shallow water and when he moved near a fish, he would kneel on the front of the boat to minimize his profile.

MORNING ALLEGIANCE - Each morning of the 2006 CITGO Bassmaster Classic hundreds of spectators gathered at Toho Marina to watch the anglers begin their day with the singing of the National Anthem.

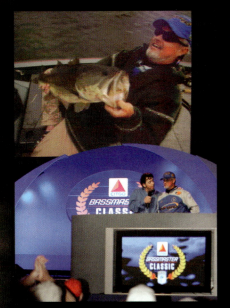

CLUNN'S EXCITEMENT - Rick Clunn, normally reserved and quiet, surprised Classic watchers by becoming visibly excited and moved when he boated a 10 pound, 10 ounce lunker on Day One.

LOCKING EXCITEMENT - While Clunn was boating his fish in Lake Toho, anglers were waiting for the lock to open to let them into one of the lakes on the Kissimmee Chain.

WEEKENDS AND BIG BASS - Jeff Coble, who represented the ESPN Outdoors Bassmaster Weekend Series anglers, weighs in. (Right) Mark Tucker holds up a 9-10 lunker, one of dozens boated during the three-day event.

5th Place
Kevin VanDam

4th Place
Terry Scroggins

Pos.	Name	Hometown	Fish	Weight	Money
1.	Luke Clausen	Spokane Valley, Wash.	15	56-02	$501,000.00
2.	Rick Morris	Lanexa, Va.	15	51-00	$45,000.00
3.	Ron Shuffield	Bismarck, Ark.	13	47-14	$40,000.00

Pos.	Name	Hometown	Fish	Weight	Money
4.	Terry Scroggins	Palatka, Fla.	15	46-15	$31,000.00
5.	Kevin VanDam	Kalamazoo, Mich.	15	44-08	$25,000.00
6.	Preston Clark	Palatka, Fla.	11	44-04	$25,000.00

3rd Place
Ron Shuffield

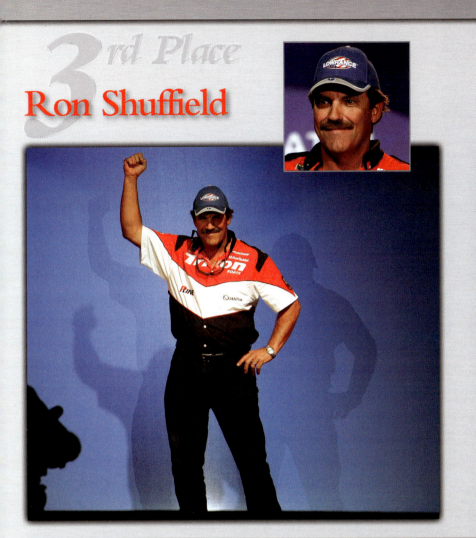

2nd Place
Rick Morris

Pos.	Name	Hometown	Fish	Weight	Money
7.	George Cochran	Hot Springs, Ark.	15	43-10	$21,500.00
8.	Kevin Wirth	Crestwood, Ky.	15	42-00	$21,000.00
9.	Jimmy Johnson	La Crosse, Wis.	15	41-14	$20,500.00

Pos.	Name	Hometown	Fish	Weight	Money
10.	Larry Nixon	Bee Branch, Ark.	15	39-13	$20,000.00
11.	Edwin Evers	Talala, Okla.	14	38-15	$15,000.00
12.	Dean Rojas	Lake Havasu, Ariz.	15	38-00	$14,500.00

Luke Clausen CHAMPION
Bassmaster Classic

COOL HAND LUKE Luke Clausen fished along the southeast shoreline of Lake Kissimmee and threw a Mann's hard-nosed, six-inch junebug plastic worm to lead all three days of the Classic.

Luke Clausen quietly stayed at the top of the standings of the CITGO Bassmaster Classic by going about his business in the same fashion all three days.

He fished along the southeast shoreline of Lake Kissimmee and threw a Mann's hard-nosed, 6-inch junebug worm to land his lunkers. The worm produced four of his five fish on the final day, including the day's biggest fish – a 5-pound, 13-ounce bass.

His ability to use a lightweight plastic in the 40-mph winds that swept across central Florida required a bit of a change to his technique.

"I kept my rod tip on the water pretty much and I would pretty much reel extremely slow and drag the worm across the bottom," Clausen said. "Because if your line gets up at all, that 40-mph wind (would be troublesome.)"

Clausen had planned to run to numerous spots on the final day. But heavy rain and wind drove him back to the spot that produced so well for him previously.

"I had a lot of confidence in the area," he said. "(During) my practice, I was in there and I had a tremendous amount of bites. I think the confidence between the bait and the area, it was hard for me to leave and go look at other spots. There were so many good fish in the area. I didn't know of any other place that could duplicate it."

VICTORY - Luke Clausen reacts after weighing in 11 pounds, 13 ounces on Day Three to secure the 2006 CITGO Bassmaster Classic title.

RECORD START - Luke Clausen proved from the start that the 2006 Classic was all his. On Day One, he weighed in the heaviest stringer in Classic history, 29 pounds, 6 ounces, anchored by these two lunkers.

CLASSIC FANS - Luke Clausen signs autographs for fans prior to launching on Day Two of the Bassmaster Classic.

Battle on the Border
∽ Lake Amistad ∽

"This lake renews your passion for fishing. It makes you forget all the small fish, all the cold mornings and all the rainy days you've ever experienced."
—Randy Howell

DEL RIO, Texas — If there was any question as to whether the CITGO Bassmaster Elite Series was truly special, it was answered in the waters of Lake Amistad in the Battle on the Border.

In essence, and strictly from a tournament-angler standpoint, this was heaven.

"This lake renews your passion for fishing," said Randy Howell by the third day of competition. "It makes you forget all the small fish, all the cold mornings and all the rainy days you've ever experienced."

In truth, though, The Battle on the Border created more unforgettable moments. At the top of that list is Ishama Monroe's victory with a four-day total of 104 pounds, 8 ounces, the second-heaviest four-day tournament weight in Bassmaster history. It was just an exclamation point for a parade of lunkers that included: 100 stringers of 20-pounds or more, 39 of those capping the 25-pound mark and another eight hitting the scales at more than 30-pounds. All of that topped off with two, four-day totals surpassing the 100-pound mark.

STARS, STRIPES AND A GOLDEN SUN - Lake Amistad produced golden sunrises that started days full of big lunkers and Mike Reynolds, who finished in third place, waving the flag on the final day.

"I saw them moving up, just swarming from the deep water."

– Fred Roumbanis

POND BASS - Pete Ponds, who finished in 14th place, promised that he would bring the largest bass of the tournament to the stage on Day Three. He did too, with an over-sized bass pillow.

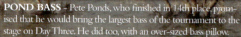

LUCKY LOUIE - Steve Kennedy had the most rabid of fans at Lake Amistad, namely his Jack Russell Terrier, Louie, sitting in Julia Kennedy's lap. When Kennedy would take the stage, Louie would bark uncontrollably.

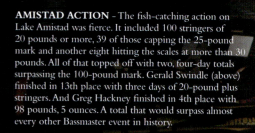

AMISTAD ACTION - The fish-catching action on Lake Amistad was fierce. It included 100 stringers of 20 pounds or more, 39 of those capping the 25-pound mark and another eight hitting the scales at more than 30 pounds. All of that topped off with two, four-day totals surpassing the 100-pound mark. Gerald Swindle (above) finished in 13th place with three days of 20-pound plus stringers. And Greg Hackney finished in 4th place with 98 pounds, 5 ounces. A total that would surpass almost every other Bassmaster event in history.

ALL AMERICAN - What could be more American? Every day started with the National Anthem and ended with big bass at the weigh-in.

5th Place
Steve Kennedy

4th Place
Greg Hackney

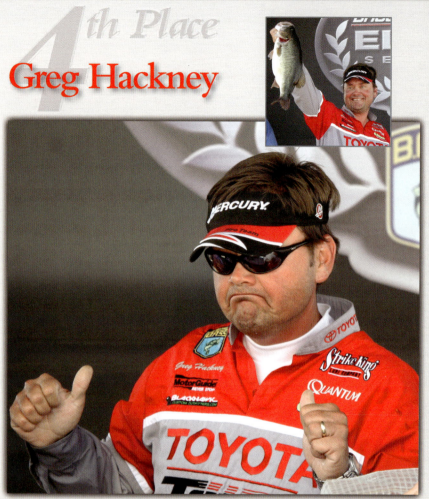

Pos.	Name	Hometown	Fish	Weight	Money
1.	Ishama Monroe	Hughson, Calif.	20	104-08	$103,000.00
2.	Fred Roumbanis	Auburn, Calif.	20	101-13	$31,000.00
3.	Mike Reynolds	Modesto, Calif.	20	99-04	$25,000.00

Pos.	Name	Hometown	Fish	Weight	Money
4.	Greg Hackney	Gonzales, La.	20	98-05	$18,000.00
5.	Steve Kennedy	Auburn, Ala.	20	97-03	$17,000.00
6.	Kevin VanDam	Kalamazoo, Mich.	20	97-00	$15,500.00

3rd Place
Mike Reynolds

2nd Place
Fred Roumbanis

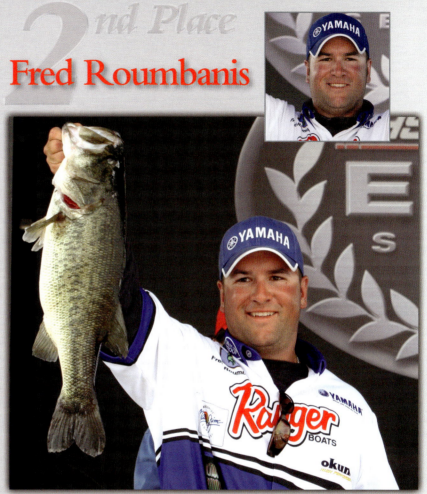

Pos.	Name	Hometown	Fish	Weight	Money
7.	Alton Jones	Waco, Texas	20	95-06	$15,000.00
8.	Gary Klein	Weatherford, Texas	20	94-03	$16,000.00
9.	Ken Cook	Lawton, Okla.	20	93-07	$15,000.00

Pos.	Name	Hometown	Fish	Weight	Money
10.	Matt Reed	Madisonville, Texas	20	91-03	$13,500.00
11.	Edwin Evers	Talala, Okla.	20	87-13	$12,500.00
12.	Dean Rojas	Lake Havasu, Ariz.	20	82-06	$12,300.00

Ishama Monroe CHAMPION

Battle on the Border

ISH WINS - Ish Monroe reacts to the realization that he had won the first CITGO Bassmaster Elite Series. He credited "a renewed focus" for allowing him to win.

BIG ISH - Ish Monroe moved into the lead of the tournament on Day Three with the largest stringer of the week, 34 pounds, 1 ounce (above) and worked his magic on Day Four with 23-8 (below) to win.

The CITGO Bassmaster Elite Series Battle on the Border was a tournament where there weren't any secrets to be figured out. It was based on tournament angling's simplest premise: Catch the most and the biggest.

Ish Monroe did that by searching for bedding fish along Amistad's shorelines and tossing a Snag Proof Tournament Frog and Reaction Innovations Vixen topwater bait in between beds to catch almost all of his fish.

Warmer temperatures spurred the spawning and pre-spawn fish into more activity. Anglers reported seeing waves of bass move to the beds, while others waiting to move were holding in deeper transition zones.

"I saw them moving up, just swarming from the deep water," said Fred Roumbanis, an Elite Series rookie, who finished second.

The combination created unreal fishing that allowed Monroe to come close to Dean Rojas's 2001 record of 108-12.

Monroe, though, put that in perspective: "The record is a piece of paper. But the win is a whole lot more."

CHAMPION-ISH – Ish Monroe searched for bedding fish along Amistad's shorelines to win. In between each bed he fished a Snag Proof Tournament Frog and Reaction Innovations Vixen topwater bait to fill out his limit and win his first Bassmaster event.

Lone Star Shootout
Sam Rayburn Reservoir

"Rayburn is without a doubt one of the best lakes in the country. It always has been. Other lakes come and go, but Rayburn has always been fairly consistent."
— Ken Cook

JASPER, Texas — A week after the first CITGO Bassmaster Elite Series, it would have been easy to make the comparison that Lake Amistad and Sam Rayburn Reservoir were like night and day. To the bass-fishing fan completely aware of the productivity of Sam Rayburn it almost seemed unfair. Since 1968, there have been 30 Bassmaster events on Sam Rayburn and almost all of them packed with excitement. This is the lake where Jim Nolan introduced the Carolina rig with an 86-pound victory in 1991 and where Randy Dearman showed the industry the value of braided line in 1993. Sam Rayburn has always set the tone for things to come.

"Rayburn is without a doubt one of the best lakes in the country," said Ken Cook. "It always has been. Other lakes come and go, but Rayburn has always been fairly consistent."

But after a week at bass fishing's newest shining light — Lake Amistad — the anglers in the CITGO Bassmaster Elite Series Lone Star Shootout presented by Triton Boats were having to make adjustments.

"It took some real adjusting the first day of practice," said Jeff Kriet. "I'd go through a place at Amistad loaded with 3-pounders and cross it off as a place to not fish because that's all it had. There have been a couple of times here I started to cross a place off my list because I wasn't getting bit every cast. That's a big adjustment."

Rayburn, though, like always, provided a look at things to come. Most notably was Greg Hackney's ability to persevere in constantly changing conditions. Hackney won the event, leading three of the four days, by methodically dead-sticking a Strike King Zero around willow trees, enticing sluggish pre-spawn and spawning bass to bite.

The tournament was marked by winds that rocked a lake known for its huge waves. That wind contributed to less-than-ideal sight-fishing conditions, making the water off-colored in some areas and producing hard-to-see-through ripples in others. Hackney, though, stuck it out blind-casting to bedding fish with a quiet confidence that was telling of even greater things to come.

BUSCH HEAVYWEIGHT - Takahiro Omori catches a keeper on Day Two (above left) that helped him win the Busch Heavyweight award with 20 pounds, 6 ounces. Omori would finish in 8th place. A line of professional anglers (above right) walk to the weigh-in stage on Day Two.

"It took some real adjusting the first day of practice. I'd go through a place at Amistad loaded with 3-pounders and cross it off as a place to not fish because that's all it had. There have been a couple of times here I started to cross a place off my list because I wasn't getting bit every cast. That's a big adjustment."

– Jeff Kriet

WURM AND KLEIN - Mike Wurm prepares his tackle prior to the start of Day Two (above left); Gary Klein visits with his daughter, Sierra, (above right) as he waits to bag his fish and head to the weigh-in.

COOL RAYBURN - The action on Sam Rayburn cooled some as compared to Lake Amistad, but the Texas reservoir still served up plenty of catches. Skeet Reese battles a keeper on Day Three (right). Reese finished in 14th place. For the record, there were nine stringers of 20 pounds or more, as compared to 100 of the same size a week earlier on Lake Amistad.

WALKING THE LINE
Tim Horton, who finished in 9th place, walks through the crowd with his final-day stringer.

GENERATIONS - Roger Hackney, father of Greg Hackney, applauds with his grandson, Drew, sitting in his lap during the final-day weigh-in at Rayburn.

5th Place
Mark Tyler

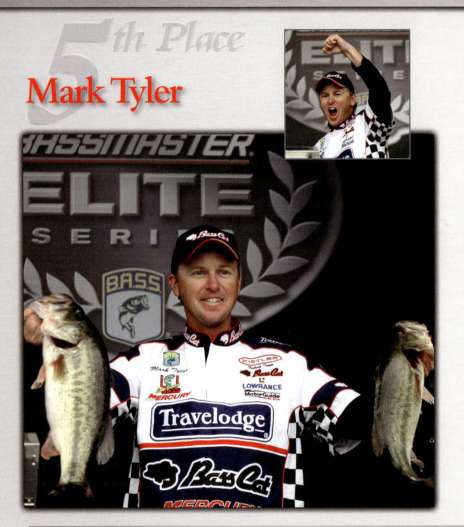

4th Place
Bill Lowen

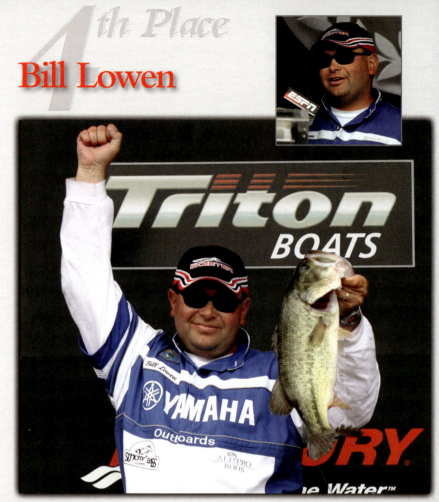

Pos.	Name	Hometown	Fish	Weight	Money
1.	Greg Hackney	Gonzales, La.	20	79-10	$102,000.00
2.	Dean Rojas	Lake Havasu, Ariz.	20	75-13	$30,000.00
3.	Kevin VanDam	Kalamazoo, Mich.	20	68-01	$25,000.00

Pos.	Name	Hometown	Fish	Weight	Money
4.	Bill Lowen	Cincinnati, Ohio	20	64-13	$18,000.00
5.	Mark Tyler	Scottsdale, Ariz.	20	64-03	$18,000.00
6.	John Crews	Salem, Va.	20	63-10	$15,500.00

3rd Place
Kevin VanDam

2nd Place
Dean Rojas

Pos.	Name	Hometown	Fish	Weight	Money
7.	Stephen Browning	Hot Springs, Ark.	20	63-01	$15,000.00
8.	Takahiro Omori	Emory, Texas	20	62-14	$15,500.00
9.	Tim Horton	Muscle Shoals, Ala.	20	61-14	$14,000.00

Pos.	Name	Hometown	Fish	Weight	Money
10.	Denny Brauer	Camdenton, Mo.	18	59-15	$13,500.00
11.	Kelly Jordon	Mineola, Texas	18	58-15	$15,500.00
12.	John Murray	Phoenix, Ariz.	20	58-07	$13,300.00

Greg Hackney CHAMPION
Lone Star Shootout

THE HACK ATTACK - Greg Hackney jumped out to a quick start by leading Day One at Rayburn, but lost fish on Day Two opened the door for others to move into the lead. By Day Three and Day Four, Hackney stopped losing fish and gained the trophy. But the biggest surprise of the day for him was his family showing up to watch him win. His wife, Julie, and sons, Drew and Luke (far, upper right) share a moment with Hackney after the final-day weigh-in.

When Greg Hackney arrived in east Texas to practice for the Lone Star Shootout presented by Triton Boats, he had a sneaking suspicion he would fare well. He was fresh off a top-five finish at Lake Amistad and was finding quality fish on Sam Rayburn Reservoir. When he seized the first-day lead, it looked like his hunch might prove true.

But on the second day of the tournament, Hackney lost a 5-pounder and a 4-pounder and fell to third place overall. Knowing every ounce counts, Hackney was worried those errors might cost him the tournament.

He was wrong.

Hackney rallied to regain the lead on Day Three.

"I guess it's really important (to be leading now), but it doesn't really matter to me," he said. "The main thing was for me to be in contention, as long as I've got a shot. So I've got just a little bit better shot now. I just fish day to day and today's another tournament. The other three days are gone."

Hackney's approach was the perfect weapon on Sam Rayburn. He finished the event with 20 bass that totaled 79 pounds, 10 ounces. He targeted shallow water near willow and cypress trees in areas that had a mix of vegetation. He worked methodically in his areas to land his lunkers on a Strike King Zero rigged weightless.

"I have to fish slow and methodical, grind it out. It's taken me all day every day," he said.

TWO FOR VICTORY - Greg Hackney holds up two of his largest fish on the final day at Rayburn. Hackney won two Busch Heavyweight awards with stringers of 22-2 and 20-8 to help him win the tournament.

Santee Cooper Showdown
Lake Moultrie & Lake Marion

"Nobody could ever dream to have a year start like this." — Preston Clark

MANNING, S.C. — If there were a record to be broken, expectations were that it would have already fallen by the time the CITGO Bassmaster Elite Series came to Santee Cooper Reservoir.

Fishing was tough in practice, according to a throng of anglers who always report tough conditions. But no one expected the wave of fish that would hit the shallows by Day One of the event. As a matter of fact, Preston Clark had only caught one keeper in three days of practice.

By the time Clark weighed in on Day One of the Santee Cooper Showdown presented by MotorGuide, three anglers had already weighed in sacks that were heavier than 30 pounds.

Clark blew those numbers out of the water. His monster bag of 39 pounds, 6 ounces was the third highest one-day total in BASS history, and would anchor a 115 pound, 15 ounce four-day total that would set the all-time heaviest winning weight.

While Clark set the record, five other anglers made a mark on the Century Club for anglers weighing in more than 100 pounds. Aaron Martens finished second with a four-day total of 108-4; Skeet Reese was third with exactly 108 pounds; Stephen Kennedy, a tour rookie, was fourth with 104-2; Kelly Jordon placed fifth with 103-3. And Dean Rojas, who presented the winner's trophy to Clark, placed sixth with 102-10.

BIG BASS SHOWDOWN - The CITGO Bassmaster Elite Series Santee Cooper Showdown was all about big bass and finding them on spawning beds. Conrad Picou, a rookie on the Elite Series, holds up a 10-pound lunker caught on Day Two. The fish was the largest weighed in during the event.

SEARCHING FOR SPAWNERS - Kelly Jordon looks for spawning fish along the edges of vegetation on Santee Cooper Reservoir. Jordon, a noted sight-fisherman, won the last contest on the lake. But he finished in 5th place at the Santee Cooper Showdown. Preston Clark concentrated his efforts in small hidden ponds to win the event and set an all-time heaviest catch record.

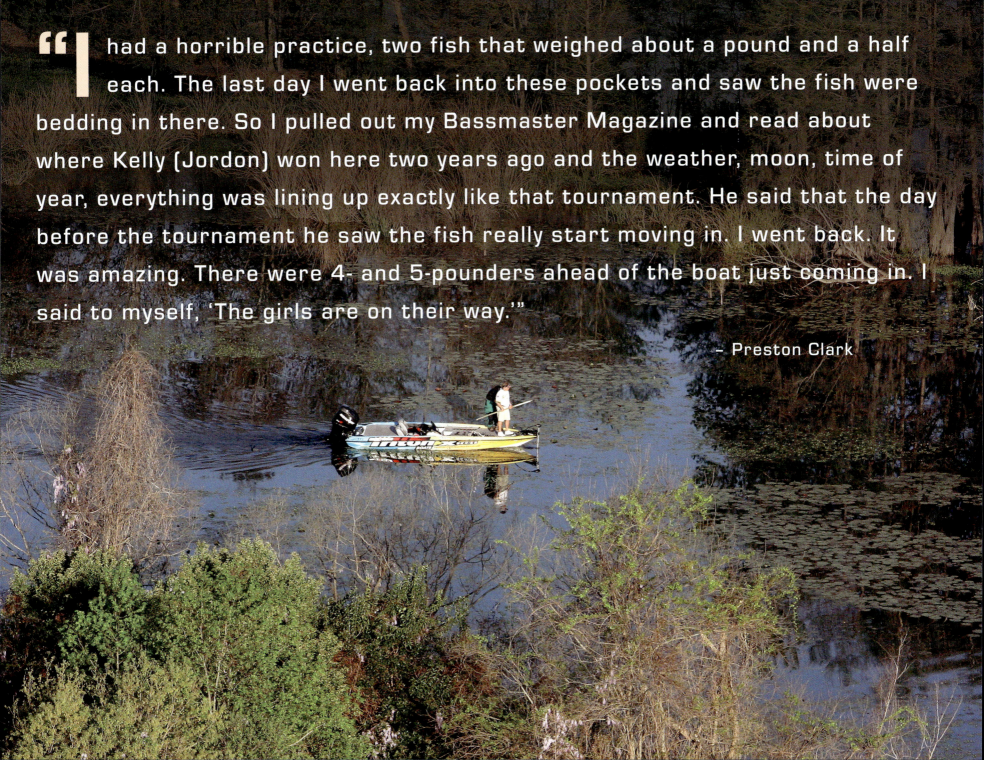

"I had a horrible practice, two fish that weighed about a pound and a half each. The last day I went back into these pockets and saw the fish were bedding in there. So I pulled out my Bassmaster Magazine and read about where Kelly (Jordon) won here two years ago and the weather, moon, time of year, everything was lining up exactly like that tournament. He said that the day before the tournament he saw the fish really start moving in. I went back. It was amazing. There were 4- and 5-pounders ahead of the boat just coming in. I said to myself, 'The girls are on their way.'"

– Preston Clark

CHECKING IN - Preston Clark checks in his Day One stringer at the bump table. None of the fish needed to be measured. The five-fish stringer totaled 39 pounds, 6 ounces.

JONES' MISFORTUNE - Alton Jones is all smiles as he gains assistance holding up a 35 pound, 6 ounce stringer. The weight would have placed Jones in 2nd place after Day One, but he was disqualified later that day for unknowingly violating a rule during the practice period.

BIG CROWDS - John Crews (above) carries his final-day stringer through the crowd at the weigh-in held at John C. Land III Landing. Crews finished the event in 9th place.

BIG WATER - Terry Scroggins (big photo left) boats his way from Lake Marion to Lake Moultrie, the two lakes that make up Santee Cooper. Scroggins finished in 7th place.

IDLE ZONE – Anglers competing on the final day of the Santee Cooper Showdown idle under a bridge, with a contingent of spectator boats, in the canal that separates Lake Marion and Lake Moultrie. Kim Wysocki (inset) holds the American flag for the playing of the National Anthem prior to the start of Day Two.

5th Place
Kelly Jordon

4th Place
Steve Kennedy

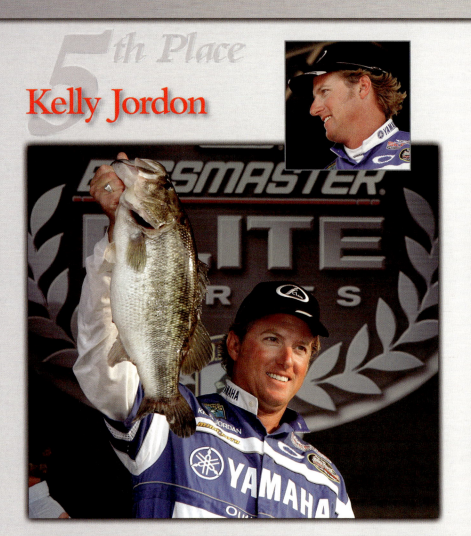

Pos.	Name	Hometown	Fish	Weight	Money
1.	Preston Clark	Palatka, Fla.	20	115-15	$101,500.00
2.	Aaron Martens	Leeds, Ala.	20	108-04	$31,500.00
3.	Skeet Reese	Auburn, Calif.	20	108-00	$25,000.00

Pos.	Name	Hometown	Fish	Weight	Money
4.	Steve Kennedy	Auburn, Ala.	20	104-02	$19,000.00
5.	Kelly Jordon	Mineola, Texas	20	103-03	$17,500.00
6.	Dean Rojas	Lake Havasu, Ariz.	20	102-10	$15,500.00

3rd Place
Skeet Reese

2nd Place
Aaron Martens

Pos.	Name	Hometown	Fish	Weight	Money
7.	Terry Scroggins	Palatka, Fla.	20	99-11	$15,000.00
8.	Kevin Wirth	Crestwood, Ky.	20	99-03	$15,500.00
9.	John Crews	Salem, Va.	20	96-03	$14,000.00

Pos.	Name	Hometown	Fish	Weight	Money
10.	Bink Desaro	Boise, Idaho	19	94-00	$13,500.00
11.	Greg Hackney	Gonzales, La.	20	91-13	$12,500.00
12.	Mike Wurm	Hot Springs, Ark.	20	86-10	$13,800.00

Preston Clark

Santee Cooper Showdown

NO WORRIES - Preston Clark started the Santee Cooper Showdown with heavy weights that needed two bags to get them to the weigh-in scales. And he continued to add to it all week, leading every day of the four-day event. But on the final day he worried that he may not have caught enough to win the event. He changed areas and caught 23 pounds, 5 ounces to win by more than seven pounds. It was the right move. Aaron Martens boated a final-day stringer of 32-10 to finish the tournament with 108 pounds, 4 ounces.

When Preston Clark started the final day of the Santee Cooper Showdown presented by Motorguide, his primary goal was to win the tournament.

If he broke the record for total weight caught over a four-day event, that would be icing on the cake.

Clark did both.

Clark's final-day 23 pounds, 5 ounces gave him a 115-pound, 15-ounce total and the record that bettered by more than seven pounds the previous four-day catch record that had been held by Dean Rojas since 2001.

"I'm just numb right now," Clark said. "I'm at a loss for words. It'll sink in on the ride home and when I watch it on TV. But I'm just excited. I'm glad it's over. I'm so relieved."

Clark had a meteoric rise in his second year on tour. He had an excellent showing at the Bassmaster Classic in February 2006 where he landed the largest bass (11 pounds, 10 ounces) in the history of the tournament. Two months later, he held the BASS tournament catch record — one of the most-coveted standards in the sport.

"No one can imagine the year I've had starting out," Clark said. "Nobody could ever dream to have a year start like this."

WALKING THE LINE - Preston Clark (above) walks past spectators, slapping their hands on the final day of the Santee Cooper Showdown. Clark receives a kiss from his daughter, Samantha (right), after he won the event. Clark said the $100,000 prize would be used to pre-pay for Samantha's college. It will certainly come in handy; Clark's wife was pregnant with triplets on the day he won.

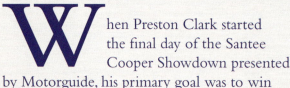

FINAL TWO - Preston Clark holds up two largemouth that helped him build a 23 pound, 5 ounce stringer on the final day of the Santee Cooper Showdown. The stringer capped an amazing week where Clark caught a four-day total of 115 pounds, 15 ounces.

THE RECORD
115 lbs. 15 oz.

Heaviest total weights in a four-day Bassmaster event

1.	Preston Clark	115-15	Santee Cooper, 2006
2.	Dean Rojas	108-15	Lake Toho, 2001
3.	Aaron Martens	108-04	Santee Cooper, 2006
4.	Skeet Reese	108-00	Santee Cooper, 2006
5.	Ishama Monroe	104-08	Lake Amistad, 2006
6.	Steve Kennedy	104-02	Santee Cooper, 2006
7.	Kelly Jordon	103-03	Santee Cooper, 2006
8.	Dean Rojas	102-10	Santee Cooper, 2006
9.	Fred Roumbanis	101-13	Lake Amistad, 2006
10.	Terry Scroggins	99-11	Santee Cooper, 2006

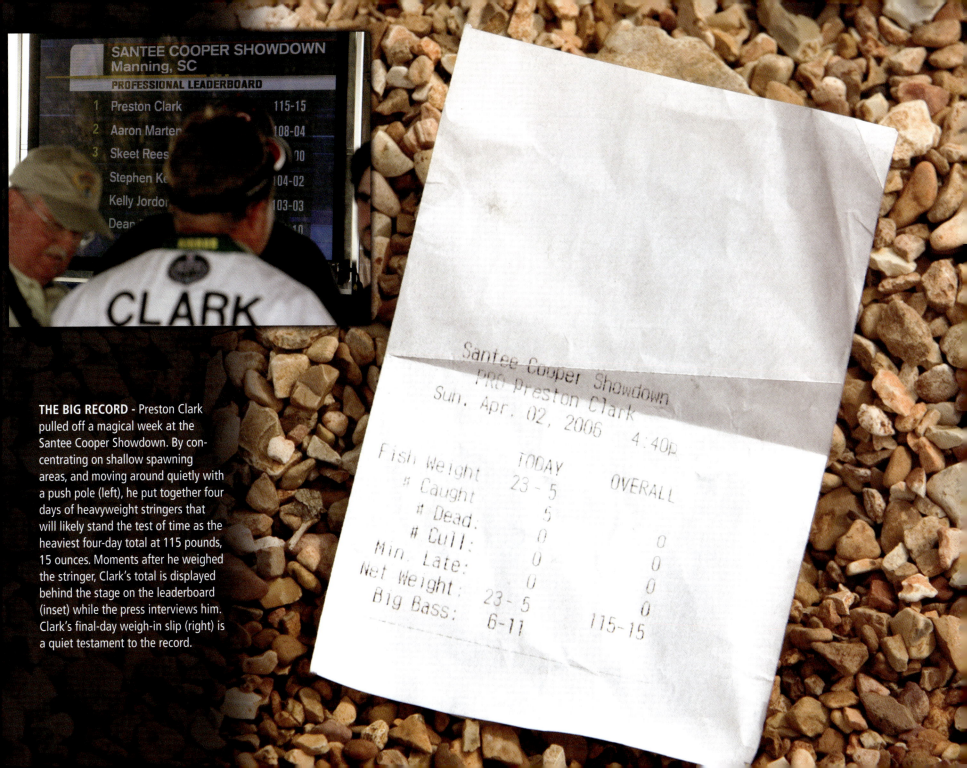

THE BIG RECORD - Preston Clark pulled off a magical week at the Santee Cooper Showdown. By concentrating on shallow spawning areas, and moving around quietly with a push pole (left), he put together four days of heavyweight stringers that will likely stand the test of time as the heaviest four-day total at 115 pounds, 15 ounces. Moments after he weighed the stringer, Clark's total is displayed behind the stage on the leaderboard (inset) while the press interviews him. Clark's final-day weigh-in slip (right) is a quiet testament to the record.

Southern Challenge
Lake Guntersville

"Things happen and you learn from your mistakes. You move on. And I think one thing with all that is my family and friends. Ish and those guys have really made me refocus. I've gotten back to what this is all about. It's about competition. It's about figuring out patterns."
— *Michael Iaconelli*

GUNTERSVILLE, Ala. — Mr. Excitement turned out to be Mr. Versatility. Michael Iaconelli, one of bass fishing's most flamboyant competitors, tried his hand at sight fishing during the final round of the CITGO Bassmaster Elite Series Southern Challenge presented by Berkley. A noted power fisherman, Iaconelli admitted sight fishing is not his favorite technique.

"I'm terrible at it," he said. But he wasn't at Guntersville.

Iaconelli finished the four-day tournament with 71 pounds, 13 ounces — giving him a narrow two-ounce victory over Alton Jones.

Then Iaconelli showed why so many fans flock to the New Jersey pro. He shouted at the top of his lungs, pumped his fists and leaped into the air several times before leaving the stage to show off two big bass to the admiring crowd.

Iaconelli said his ability to adapt to a myriad of fishing conditions on Lake Guntersville propelled him to victory. There were periods of intense rain followed by intense sunshine and fluctuating temperatures.

When the sun shined brightly on the final day, and Iaconelli only had two fish in his live well, he made the move to the shoreline where he began sight fishing.

"It's the hardest thing in the world (to leave a good spot)," he said. "In the past, I've had several good tournaments here where I committed to an area and I died on it. So at 11:30 today, I decided to go back up and go shallow to sight fish. It paid off. I've got to tell you, that decision is what won it for me. That and not giving up."

LIGHTS ON THE WATER - Competitors in the CITGO Bassmaster Elite Series Southern Challenge on Lake Guntersville gather at the take-off point with their running lights creating a shimmering trail in the pre-dawn.

IKE PREVAILS - Michael Iaconelli had led two other Bassmaster events on Lake Guntersville going into the final day but faltered and dropped out of contention. In 2006, Iaconelli made all the right moves to win.

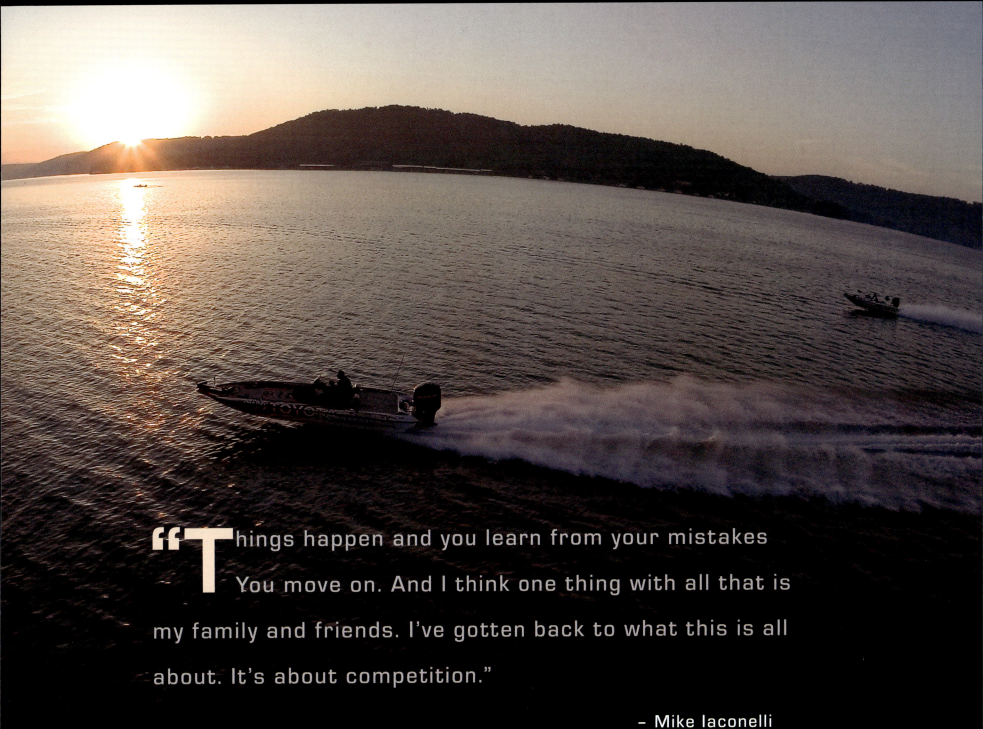

"Things happen and you learn from your mistakes You move on. And I think one thing with all that is my family and friends. I've gotten back to what this is all about. It's about competition."

– Mike Iaconelli

WBT CHAMP - Tammy Richardson (below) of Amity, Ark., holds up the Mercury Women's Bassmaster Tour presented by Triton Boats (WBT) trophy after she became the first winner of the new trail. The WBT competed on nearby Neely Henry and weighed in prior to the Day Three Elite Series weigh-in.

BLURRY BRAUER - Denny Brauer passes by the checkout dock during take off of the CITGO Bassmaster Elite Series Southern Challenge. Brauer finished in 16th in the event.

RAIN DELAY - Huge crowds were a constant part of the Southern Challenge, but on Day One a thunderstorm rolled through the area, scattering spectators and anglers and forcing a delay in the weigh-in for about 30 minutes.

MOWING GRASS - Lake Guntersville is synonymous with thick grass like the thick mat that John Crews was forced to clean from his trolling motor during Day Two of the CITGO Bassmaster Elite Series Southern Challenge.

SWEET HOME ALABAMA - Gerald Swindle (Right) always fares well on Lake Guntersville. The Alabama pro finished in 5th overall.

5th Place — Gerald Swindle

4th Place — Kevin VanDam

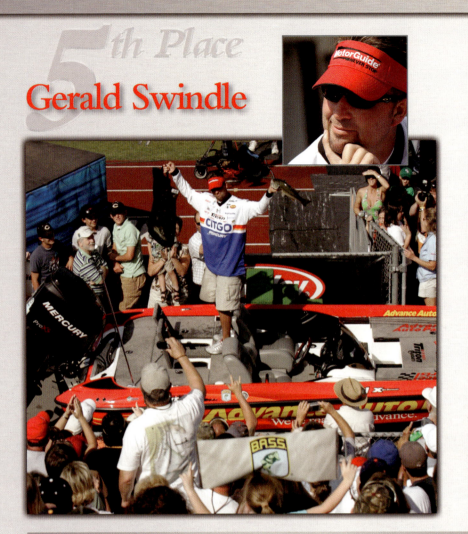
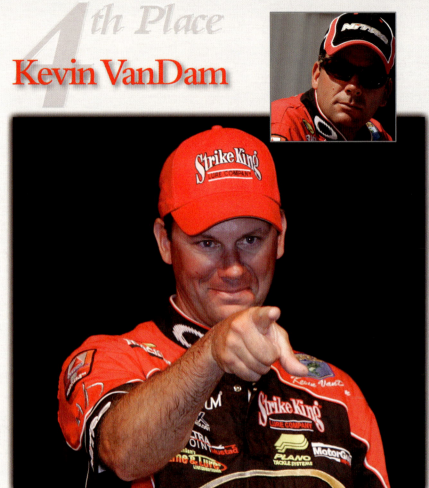

Pos.	Name	Hometown	Fish	Weight	Money
1.	Michael Iaconelli	Runnemede, N.J.	20	71-13	$101,000.00
2.	Alton Jones	Waco, Texas	20	71-11	$30,000.00
3.	Steve Kennedy	Auburn, Ala.	20	69-08	$26,000.00

Pos.	Name	Hometown	Fish	Weight	Money
4.	Kevin VanDam	Kalamazoo, Mich.	20	66-13	$18,000.00
5.	Gerald Swindle	Warrior, Ala.	20	66-05	$18,000.00
6.	Takahiro Omori	Emory, Texas	19	65-10	$15,500.00

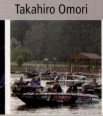

3rd Place
Steve Kennedy

2nd Place
Alton Jones

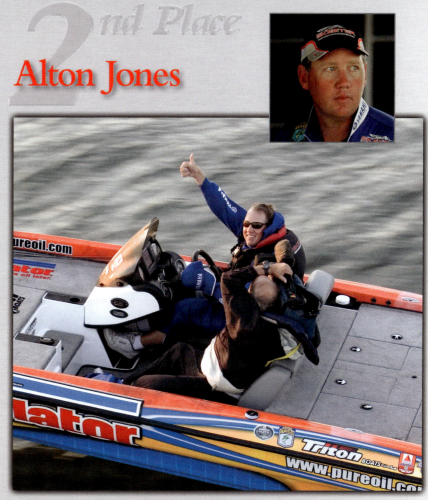

Pos.	Name	Hometown	Fish	Weight	Money
7.	Edwin Evers	Talala, Okla.	20	62-01	$15,000.00
8.	Mark Tucker	St. Louis, Mo.	19	60-00	$14,500.00
9.	Jeff Reynolds	Idabel, Okla.	17	57-02	$15,000.00

Pos.	Name	Hometown	Fish	Weight	Money
10.	Timmy Horton	Muscle Shoals, Ala.	17	56-13	$13,500.00
11.	Dean Rojas	Lake Havasu, Ariz.	17	55-08	$12,500.00
12.	Yusuke Miyazaki	Mineola, Texas	16	52-05	$12,300.00

Mike Iaconelli
CHAMPION
Southern Challenge

IKE GOES IKE - Mike Iaconelli barely edged Alton Jones by two ounces to win the CITGO Bassmaster Elite Series Southern Challenge on Lake Guntersville. And it was a cause for an Ike-style celebration. With these two fish in hand, he jumped off the stage and ran into the crowd.

IKE GOES TO BED - Mike Iaconelli is considered a power fisherman, but at Guntersville he switched things up and spent part of his time sight fishing for bedding bass. It worked. Iaconelli caught the Busch Heavyweight on Day Two (below) to put him in position to win.

It was a familiar scene on Lake Guntersville – Mike Iaconelli in the lead. Iaconelli had held the lead twice before in Bassmaster tournaments on Lake Guntersville. But both times, Iaconelli failed to collect a win.

That scene started to get real familiar for Iaconelli. The flamboyant pro had only two fish in his livewell, when he made a critical move to the shallow shoreline and began sight fishing. It was the perfect move. He boated three keepers in the final minutes and won the CITGO Bassmaster Elite Series Southern Challenge by a scant two ounces.

Iaconelli caught his winning fish using a Berkley Power Noodle that he fished weightless, but altered by sticking a finishing nail on the lure's tail. "It gave it a reverse fall," he said. "I threw it on 8-pound fluorocarbon. It was just pure finesse."

"With three minutes to go, I spotted a fish that was guarding fry," he said. "I spun the boat around. I set the hook, landed it and measured it. By the time I was done, I looked at my watch and I had one minute to go before I had to run back. That was the winning fish."

LIKE IKE - Mike Iaconelli, one of the most loved and hated of professional anglers, was anxious to put a disqualification at the 2006 CITGO Bassmaster Classic behind him. He said his season was one of a renewed focus of trying to get back to the basics of fishing. His victory at Guntersville was a result of that renewed focus. The closeness of the competition (only two ounces separated him and Alton Jones) with the huge crowds (right) set up an exciting finish at the CITGO Bassmaster Elite Series Southern Challenge on Lake Guntersville.

Pride of Augusta
～ Clarks Hill ～

"It meant a whole lot, knowing the places the herring like to spawn and the type of points where they like to spawn this time of year definitely helped. I've actually stumbled before in tournaments when I knew a lot about the lake and was trying to fish memories. But that didn't happen here."
— *Davy Hite*

AUGUSTA, Ga. — After four straight events where sight fishing was the cornerstone of the season's action, the CITGO Bassmaster Elite Series Pride of Augusta presented by Lowrance was supposed to be a welcome relief from the annual spawn.

It didn't quite pan out that way. The bass weren't spawning, but the blueback herring were. And on Clarks Hill Lake that transformed this tournament into an event where anglers chased big schools of baitfish also being chased by schools of largemouth.

Davy Hite won the chase. He weighed in a four-day total of 71 pounds, 12 ounces to capture the title by almost nine pounds.

The final-day backdrop of the convincing victory was one of rain, clouds and slight winds. Conventional wisdom indicated it was the perfect conditions for one of the trailing anglers to make up lost ground, but not on Clarks Hill or with bluebacks.

"Most of the guys are used to fishing lakes where shad is the main forage," said Jason Quinn. "When you have those weather conditions, you can key in on those shad and catch them a lot easier on topwaters. Unfortunately, this is a blueback herring lake. That's the main forage here. When those bluebacks move, those bass want to be coming up and busting them."

"The bluebacks like to get up on top of the water, but they need that sun to get up. Once it does, the bass will get up there and run the herrings. (Inclement) weather keeps the bluebacks down a bit. And the bass don't feed as well."

Hite, though, concentrated on areas where he knew the bluebacks liked to spawn, riding those areas to the top of the standings.

THE PRIDE - Kenyon Hill runs across Clarks Hill on the final day with an ESPN cameraman capturing the action (above) and Davy Hite, champion of the event, holds up two keepers caught on the final day.

"I've said this before, but I have bombed in a tournament because of the knowledge I have of the lake. I had an advantage this week because I know the lake really well, and I know the places the herring like to congregate on. You know, I also had a bait that not many people chose. I told Kevin (VanDam) in practice that I was getting a few bites on that big jig, and they always make fun of it. I think he was throwing one yesterday."

– Davy Hite

FATHER'S PRIDE - Aaron Martens holds his favorite keeper, daughter Jordan after Day Two's weigh-in.

TAKE OFF - Competitors in the CITGO Bassmaster Elite Series Pride of Augusta file past the check-out dock on Day Two of the event.

FINALISTS WAIT - (Above photo) Mark Tucker (left), Gary Klein (center) and Peter Thliveros (right) hold their weigh-in bags while waiting for their chance to weigh in at Clarks Hill Lake. While they waited, a big crowd gathered (right photo) despite threatening clouds that had produced thunderstorms off and on all day. (Right) Keith Alan, Bassmaster Elite Series emcee, fires up the crowd prior to the start of the weigh-in. Luckily, the rain held off long enough to finish the weigh-in.

CHASING THE BLUES – A largemouth jumps out of the water and onto a cruising blueback herring during the final day of the Pride of Augusta, while Davy Hite looks on.

5th Place Randy Howell

4th Place Kevin Wirth

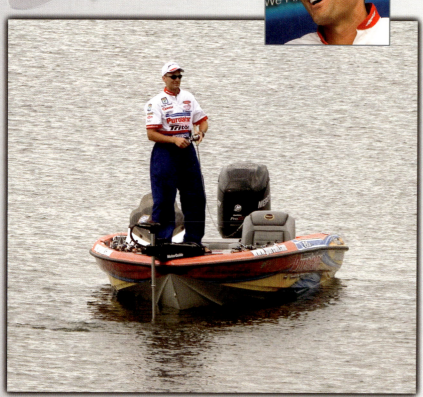

Pos.	Name	Hometown	Fish	Weight	Money
1.	Davy Hite	Ninety Six, S.C.	20	71-12	$100,000.00
2.	Kenyon Hill	Norman, Okla.	20	62-15	$32,000.00
3.	Jason Quinn	York, S.C.	20	60-10	$25,000.00

Pos.	Name	Hometown	Fish	Weight	Money
4.	Kevin Wirth	Crestwood, Ky.	20	59-12	$18,000.00
5.	Randy Howell	Springville, Ala.	20	58-07	$18,000.00
6.	Mark Tucker	St Louis, Mo.	20	57-00	$15,500.00

3rd Place
Jason Quinn

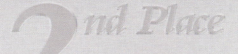

2nd Place
Kenyon Hill

Pos.	Name	Hometown	Fish	Weight	Money
7.	Jared Lintner	Arroyo Grande, Calif.	20	55-07	$15,000.00
8.	Peter Thliveros	Jacksonville, Fla.	20	55-02	$14,500.00
9.	Jeff Reynolds	Idabel, Okla.	20	54-05	$14,000.00

Pos.	Name	Hometown	Fish	Weight	Money
10.	John Crews	Salem, Va.	20	54-04	$13,500.00
11.	Gary Klein	Weatherford, Texas	20	53-09	$12,500.00
12.	Michael Iaconelli	Runnemede, N.J.	20	53-02	$13,300.00

Davy Hite
CHAMPION
Pride of Augusta

SPECIAL VICTORY - Davy Hite has won two Bassmaster Angler of the Year titles and a Bassmaster Classic. But he said his victory at the Clarks Hill was special because he was able to enjoy it with family, including his sons Parker and Peyton (right), who help him hold up his champion's trophy while his wife, Natalie, looks on.

Prior to the Pride of Augusta presented by Lowrance, Davy Hite had won two Bassmaster Angler of the Year titles and a Bassmaster Classic.

But even with those accomplishments already in tow, he said his victory at Clarks Hill Lake is among his most cherished moments as a professional fisherman.

Hite clinched the tournament with a four-day total of 71 pounds, 12 ounces. The victory was made extra-special by the fact that Hite lives in Ninety Six, S.C., only 40 minutes from Clarks Hill Lake. Friends and family were on hand to cheer for him throughout the four tough days of angling, including the final day's heavy thunderstorms.

"This is just great," Hite said. "It's just awesome. That weather was so awful. It was dangerous. But I had fans that wanted to stay out there with me."

Hite began each day in the Parksville area with a 1/2-ounce brown Buckeye jig, then would move up the Georgia Little River and King Creek later in the day. The pattern, one he first used in a Federation tournament two decades earlier, fell off a bit in the final round because of the inclement weather, so Hite used a variety of 4- and 5-inch swimbaits to pick up the pace.

LAUNCH TO TAKE OFF - Davy Hite wasn't fishing home water. But it was close to home. Hite lives in Ninety Six, S.C., just 40 miles from the lake.

He said his knowledge of the habits of the blueback herring provided an edge. "It meant a whole lot," he said, "knowing the places the herring like to spawn and the type of points where they like to spawn this time of year definitely helped. I've actually stumbled before in tournaments when I knew a lot about the lake and was trying to fish memories. But that didn't happen here."

NOT SO DANGEROUS - Davy Hite fishes a shallow water hump, so shallow that it includes a "Danger" sign. It was one of Hite's honey holes during the Pride of Augusta, where he tossed a Buckeye jig and swimbait to largemouth chasing blueback herring.

Bassmaster Memorial

Eagle Mountain Lake & Benbrook Lake

"(Day Three) is when the tournament was won. Today was kind of just hanging on."

— *Peter Thliveros*

FORT WORTH, Texas — The Bassmaster Memorial was all about dreams. Peter Thliveros won the event just days after having a dream that showed him winning a tournament.

He wasn't certain which tournament it was, but he clearly remembered that he finished first and his fellow Elite angler Edwin Evers finished second.

Well, the dream turned out to be only half true.

Evers wound up finishing third in the inaugural Bassmaster Major. Thliveros, on the other hand, claimed victory in the tour's first major and collected the $250,000 first prize that accompanied the win.

Thliveros, a Jacksonville, Fla., resident and a 17-year tour veteran, caught a total of 25 pounds, 8 ounces which easily topped the other five anglers who survived two different cuts to fish for the Memorial championship.

Michael Iaconelli finished second with a two-day total of 22 pounds, 3 ounces. Evers finished in third with 20 pounds, 4 ounces. Both Thliveros and Iaconelli passed the $1 million mark in career BASS earnings at the Memorial. But while those were milestones for both anglers, the day clearly belonged to Thliveros.

"This is by far the most prestigious victory I've ever had," Thliveros said. "My first victory was obviously tremendous. Last year, after a nine-year dry spell, winning then was like winning the first one all over again. But this one is just the most prestigious event I've ever been in."

BIG WAVES AND BIG BASS - Michael Iaconelli (above) cuts a path across a choppy Benbrook Lake during the Bassmaster Memorial on Day Four, while Peter Thliveros (left), the champion of the event holds up a 7-pound largemouth caught on Day Three.

"This is by far the most prestigious victory I've ever had. My first victory was obviously tremendous. Last year, after a nine-year dry spell, winning then was like winning the first one all over again. But this one is just the most prestigious event I've ever been in."
— Peter Thliveros

HOLE-TO-HOLE – Mark Menendez changes holes during the final round of the Bassmaster Memorial on Benbrooke Lake. Menendez finished 4th in the event.

FISHING RODEO – The competitors in the Bassmaster Memorial held their angler meeting in the legendary rodeo arena of Billy Bob's in Fort Worth, Texas.

CLARK WINS Dianna Clark holds up two largemouth that helped her capture the Mercury Women's Bassmaster Tour presented by Triton Boats title at Lake Lewisville. The event was held in conjunction with the Major.

MAJOR REESE – Skeet Reese fishes on Benbrook Lake on Day Three of the Bassmaster Memorial. Reese finished in 5th place.

SPECTATORS GALORE – Even though Benbrooke Lake was small, spectators turned out in droves to follow their favorite anglers, including this armada following Mike Iaconelli on Day Four.

THE FINALISTS - The final 12 anglers in the Bassmaster Memorial were (left to right, back row) Dave Wolak, Skeet Reese, Peter Thliveros, Todd Faircloth, Greg Hackney, Edwin Evers, Mark Menendez and Randy Howell. (Front row, left to right) Michael Iaconelli, Matt Reed, John Crews and Mike McClelland.

FINAL START - The final six anglers idle out to the six-hole course on Benbrook Lake on Day Four of the Bassmaster Memorial. The anglers were required to fish the pre-designated areas on the lake for 1 hour, 10 minutes before moving to the next hole.

5th Place — Skeet Reese

4th Place — Mark Menendez

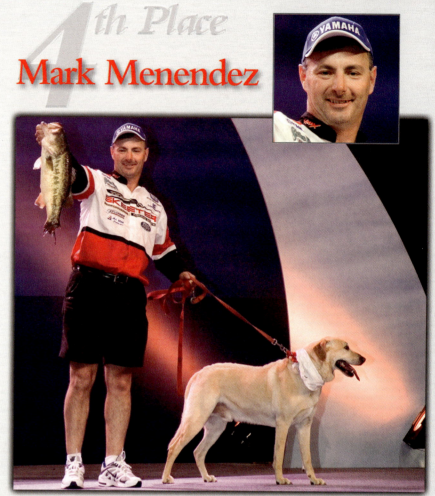

Pos.	Name	Hometown	Fish	Weight	Money
1.	Peter Thliveros	Jacksonville, Fla.	8	25-08	$255,000.00
2.	Michael Iaconelli	Runnemede, N.J.	9	22-03	$33,500.00
3.	Edwin Evers	Talala, Okla.	8	20-04	$28,500.00

Pos.	Name	Hometown	Fish	Weight	Money
4.	Mark Menendez	Paducah, Ky.	6	17-14	$22,000.00
5.	Skeet Reese	Auburn, Calif.	6	14-04	$20,000.00
6.	Greg Hackney	Gonzales, La.	4	9-13	$17,000.00

3rd Place
Edwin Evers

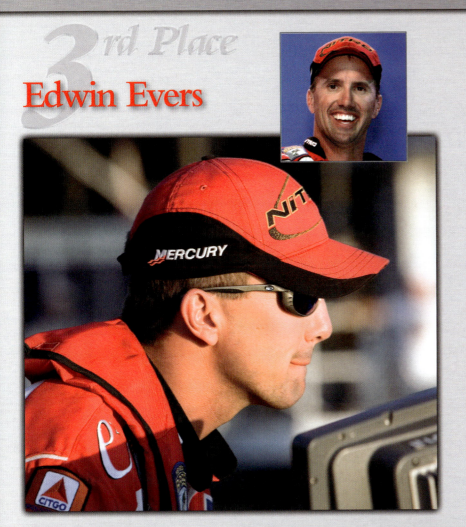

2nd Place
Mike Iaconelli

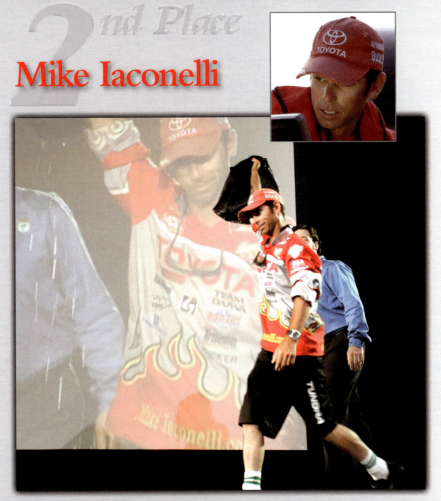

Pos.	Name	Hometown	Fish	Weight	Money
7.	Mike McClelland	Bella Vista, Ark.	3	7-00	$16,500.00
8.	Todd Faircloth	Jasper, Texas	2	4-11	$16,000.00
9.	Dave Wolak	Warrior Run, Pa.	2	4-06	$16,500.00

Pos.	Name	Hometown	Fish	Weight	Money
10.	Randy Howell	Springville, Ala.	1	4-02	$15,000.00
11.	John Crews	Salem, Va.	2	4-00	$13,100.00
12.	Matt Reed	Madisonville, Texas	0	0-00	$13,000.00

DAM IT ALL – Peter Thliveros won the Bassmaster Memorial by concentrating on riprap dams on Eagle Mountain Lake and Benbrook Lake. The dams were so productive they produced Purolator Big Bass for Thliveros on Day Two and Day Three.

Peter Thliveros
CHAMPION
Bassmaster Memorial

COOKING UP A WIN
Prior to his Bassmaster career, Peter Thliveros was a chef in his father's Italian restaurant. By the time he hit the Bassmaster Trail he started heating things up, bringing a fiery competitive streak that is evident in his face moments after winning the Bassmaster Memorial.

My how things can change in a Bassmaster event. Going into the Bassmaster Memorial, Peter Thliveros had little if any confidence of doing well. By Day Three, he was so firmly in command the rest of the competition knew it was his to lose.

Thliveros won the event in convincing fashion, outdistancing Michael Iaconelli by 3 pounds. The change in confidence came after Thliveros landed the biggest bass of both Day's Two and Three with lunkers eclipsing the 7-pound mark.

For the first three days of the Memorial (the first two on Eagle Mountain Lake and the third on Benbrook Lake), Thliveros found his best fish along rock dams using a 1/2-ounce Team Supreme Ultimate Rattling Rascal jig. But the dam didn't produce the fish Thliveros was looking for on the final day. So he switched to a 3/8-ounce Team Supreme jig and the fish began to bite.

"All I did was change the presentation from pitching and flipping techniques to casting," Thliveros said. "I continued to fish the big heavy jig on the rock dam the way I'd been doing it, but I just didn't catch the fish off it. The other fish came casting. I was fishing little rough points, little flat points with gravel rock on it and some trees underwater that I couldn't see is actually where I caught (some of my fish.)"

With the unexpected change to his pattern, Thliveros said he had to scramble on Day Four to maintain his lead.

"The last day of practice is when I figured out the pattern on Eagle Mountain and what got me to this," Thliveros said. "(Day Three) is when the tournament was won. Today was kind of just hanging on."

THE DIFFERENCE A DAY MAKES
Peter Thliveros started the Bassmaster Memorial with a complete lack of confidence. But he fared well enough to make the top-12 on Eagle Mountain Lake, and after moving to Benbrook Lake he took complete control. On Day Three he caught enough fish to almost ensure victory and in the final he capped it off, winning $250,000 and moving into the Bassmaster Millionaire's Club.

FIREWORKS
Peter Thliveros stands in the middle of a fireworks show during the final-day weigh-in at the Bassmaster Memorial. Thliveros won the tournament in convincing fashion and with the $250,000 first place check moved his career earnings over the $1 million mark.

Sooner Run
∞ Grand Lake ∞

"These post-spawn fish want a very, very slow presentation. I'd drag my bait... yo-yo it until one of those big ones latched on."
— Mike McClelland

GROVE, Okla. — Mike McClelland gave a new meaning to the word "dominance" in the CITGO Bassmaster Elite Series Sooner Run on Grand Lake.

From Day One, McClelland took charge of the event, leading Day One by two ounces, opening up the lead to 12 pounds on Day Two and never looked back, winning the event with 79 pounds, 7 ounces. That total was 15 pounds, 9 ounces ahead of his closest competitor.

"This is surreal," McClelland said.

Part of that feeling was from a $100,000 first-place paycheck. But more importantly, it may prove to be the next step up the ladder of professional bass fishing success for McClelland. He started fishing Bassmaster events in 1997, then quit the pro circuit for two years while working for Champion Boats before returning to the tour in 2004.

McClelland has tasted success before. He had won three Bassmaster tournaments before this season, including the 2005 CITGO Bassmaster Open Championship on the Alabama River.

"Before this season, my goal was to win the (Bassmaster) Classic, Angler of the Year or one of these Elite Series tournaments," said McClelland. "I feel like I've reached that next plateau now. This solidifies me as an angler who is going to remain on the Tour."

OZARK SUNRISE - The Ozark Mountains surrounding Grand Lake provided some spectacular sunrises and picturesque takeoffs in an event that Mike McClelland (left and far right) took command of early and never relented.

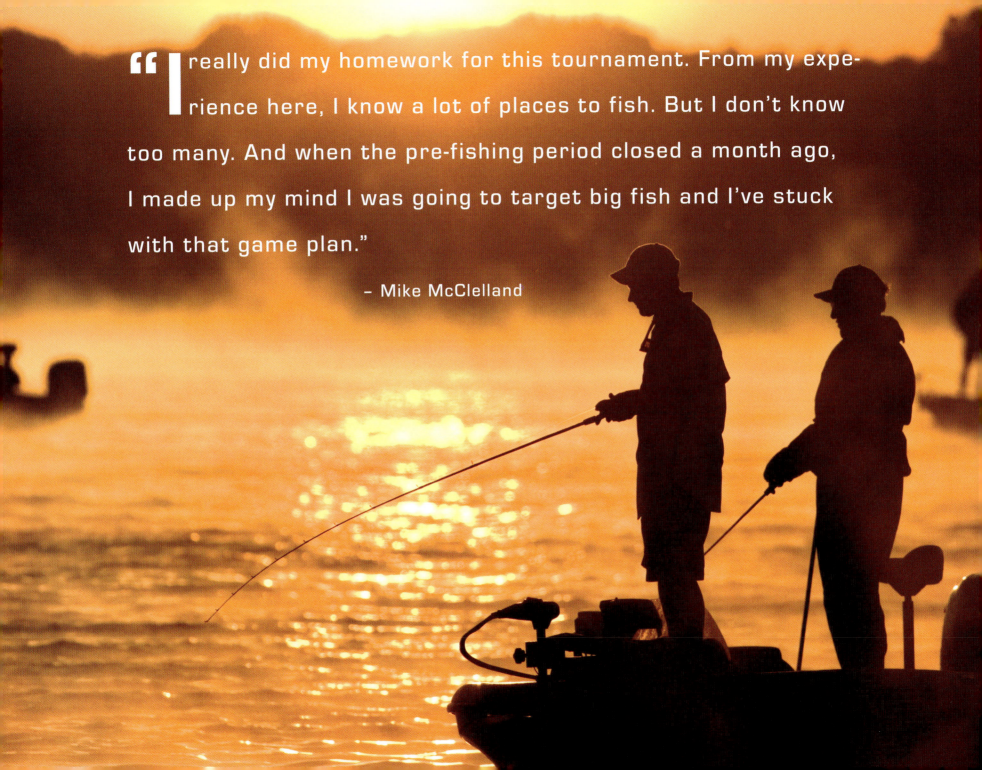

"I really did my homework for this tournament. From my experience here, I know a lot of places to fish. But I don't know too many. And when the pre-fishing period closed a month ago, I made up my mind I was going to target big fish and I've stuck with that game plan."

– Mike McClelland

GRAND LINEUP – A line of competitor boats (above left) sit against the dock during the weigh-in of the CITGO Bassmaster Elite Series Sooner Run on Grand Lake. This was the first season BASS required anglers to wrap their boats in sponsor colors and logos. The event was primarily centered around anglers fishing along deep structure, but Dean Rojas (above) strayed from the norm and concentrated on shallow logs and willows with his signature topwater frog, Kermit. Rojas finished in 5th place. Michael Iaconelli (left) fights a spotted bass caught off a deep point near the takeoff on Day Two, while the sun rises and spectators gather behind Mike McClelland (lower left).

ROOKIE BREAKOUT – Jeff Connella, a rookie on the Elite Series, (below) had a breakout tournament at Grand Lake that included a following of fans (above). Connella finished in 7th place.

5th Place
Dean Rojas

4th Place
Edwin Evers

Pos.	Name	Hometown	Fish	Weight	Money
1.	Mike McClelland	Bella Vista, Ark.	20	79-07	$104,000.00
2.	Matt Reed	Madisonville, Texas	20	63-14	$31,000.00
3.	Greg Gutierrez	Red Bluff, Calif.	20	63-00	$26,000.00

Pos.	Name	Hometown	Fish	Weight	Money
4.	Edwin Evers	Talala, Okla.	20	57-07	$18,000.00
5.	Dean Rojas	Lake Havasu, Ala.	19	57-05	$18,000.00
6.	Paul Elias	Laufel, Miss.	20	57-02	$15,500.00

3rd Place — Greg Gutierrez

2nd Place — Matt Reed

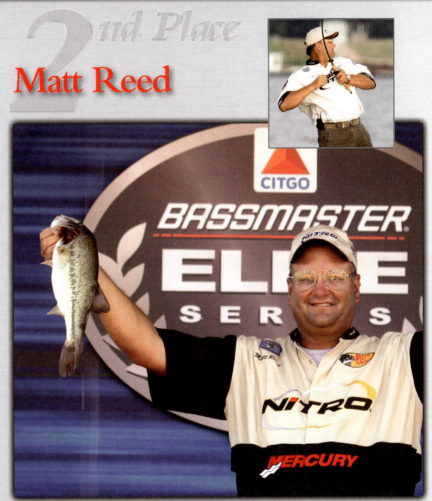

Pos.	Name	Hometown	Fish	Weight	Money
7.	Jeff Connella	Bentley, La.	20	56-12	$15,000.00
8.	Ken Cook	Lawton, Okla.	20	56-08	$14,500.00
9.	Aaron Martens	Leeds, Ala.	20	56-01	$14,000.00

Pos.	Name	Hometown	Fish	Weight	Money
10.	Michael Iaconelli	Runnemede, N.J.	20	54-15	$13,500.00
11.	Chad Brauer	Osage Beach, Mo.	20	54-12	$12,500.00
12.	Jami Fralick	Martin, S.D.	19	54-09	$12,300.00

Mike McClelland
Sooner Run

CLOSE TO HOME - Mike McClelland credited the victory at Grand Lake with his knowledge of the fishery. The Arkansas pro lives 1 hour from the lake and its proximity produced a large crowd of family and fans, most wearing yellow T-shirts with "Yellin' for McClelland" printed on them. The fans included his wife, Stacy (right).

GRAND MCCLELLAND - Mike McClelland won the Sooner Run by concentrating for larger bass on deep structure. The tactic worked well enough for him to win the Purolator Big Bass award two of four days of the event.

Two weeks earlier, when Mike McClelland finished seventh in the Bassmaster Memorial in Fort Worth, Texas, he missed the cut for the final day, and therefore a chance to win, by three ounces. McClelland typically has a large entourage of family and friends that travels from Arkansas to support him, some wearing "Yellin' for McClelland" T-shirts. When they consoled him after the close-but-no-cigar performance at Fort Worth, McClelland told every one of them the same thing.

"I told them it was okay," recalled McClelland, "but I really want to win at Grand Lake."

McClelland, a 38-year-old Bella Vista, Ark., resident, not only won the CITGO Bassmaster Elite Series Sooner Run on Grand Lake, he led from start to finish. And it wasn't even close.

"This is where I learned to fish boat docks, and this lake is where I learned to flip willow trees," McClelland said. "I learned a lot about fishing deep structure on this lake, too."

That last technique is what McClelland relied on to win this week. "The biggest thing I did was slow down," McClelland said. "These post-spawn fish want a very, very slow presentation. I'd drag my bait until I hit a brushpile. When I'd get it there, I'd just yo-yo it until one of those big ones latched on."

MCCLELLAND'S TIME - Elite Series' fans gather around Mike McClelland moments after he won the Sooner Run on Grand Lake. McClelland signed hats, T-shirts and a copy of BASS Times, featuring him on the cover after he won the Bassmaster Open Championship in December of 2005.

Bluegrass Brawl
Kentucky Lake

"Unbelievable and awesome. A dream come true." — *Morizo Shimizu*

GILBERTSVILLE, Ky. — Kevin Wirth held the lead and Kevin VanDam held the star power. But after the final round of the CITGO Bassmaster Elite Series Bluegrass Brawl, Morizo Shimizu held the trophy.

Shimizu, the 35-year-old native of Osaka, Japan, overcame driving rains and powerful wind gusts to clinch his first CITGO Bassmaster Elite Series victory with a four-day total of 66 pounds, 9 ounces.

"Unbelievable and awesome," Shimizu said to the crowd shortly after winning. "A dream come true."

Shimizu carried on the tradition of foreign-born anglers faring well on this massive Tennessee River impoundment. Norio Tanabe, also of Japan, became the first international BASS event winner when the last tournament was held here in 1993.

Wirth, a Kentucky native and a pre-tournament favorite to win the event, was seeking his first BASS victory in more than 11 years, but fell short in his effort. He finished with a 13-pound, 9-ounce limit and took second place with a 64-14 total. VanDam was third with 63-8.

"There hadn't been a 20-pound sack all week and he came up with one today," Wirth said of Shimizu. "I knew if they caught them at all I was in trouble. They were really the only two guys that could beat me and one of the two caught them. So, he did an outstanding job."

"I was fishing in 10 to 16 feet of water," Shimizu said through an interpreter. "I have fished this lake before with another tournament and I know a lot of fish can be caught far away. Usually, I would run 40 minutes or more to catch fish. But this tournament, I looked for closer areas to catch fish. I pre-fished a tournament two or three years ago at Moors Creek and had a big fish over there. I had a feeling I would have a big fish again in that area."

TWO EXTREMES - Kentucky Lake required a multifaceted approach, like the one Skeet Reese used to finish in 4th place. Reese fished drops like this one near a bridge. One minute he would be casting the monster-sized 10-inch plastic worm, and the next finessing with a drop-shot rig. Reese almost decided not to fish the final day because his wife, Kim, was due to go into labor that day.

BIG MAMAS - Morizo Shimizu holds up two largemouth bass that he called "Big Mamas." The two fish helped him build a 19-pound, 3-ounce stringer on Day Two, launching him from 49th place on Day One into 10th place on Day Two. The Japanese angler would continue to climb the standings to win the Bluegrass Brawl, edging past local favorite Kevin Wirth (right) who led the event going into the final day.

"There hadn't been a 20-pound sack all week and (Morizo Shimizu) came up with one today. I knew if they (VanDam, Shimizu) caught them at all I was in trouble. They were really the only two guys that could beat me and one of the two caught them. So, he did an outstanding job."

– Kevin Wirth

OLD GLORY - Every day of every CITGO Bassmaster Elite Series started with anglers standing for the singing of the National Anthem. It was the traditional kick-off. Once the anthem was over, the first boat was put into motion for take-off.

KRIET'S PLACE - Jeff Kriet holds up a largemouth he caught during the Bluegrass Brawl on Kentucky Lake. Kriet finished the event in 6th place.

CATCHING ONE - Kevin Wirth battles a keeper he caught on Day Three of the Bluegrass Brawl. Wirth, a local favorite, led the event going into the final day, but Morizo Shimizu's final-day weight of 20 pounds, 6 ounces was too much to overcome.

KISS FOR DAD - Joe Thomas receives a kiss from his daughter after the weigh-in on Day Two of the Bluegrass Brawl. The event was held on Father's Day weekend.

FATHER'S DAY - It was Father's Day on the final of the Bluegrass Brawl and Kevin VanDam got to enjoy it with his twin sons, Jackson and Nicholas.

ALL IN THE FAMILY - Jimmy Mize (right) poses with his wife, Lucy (left), and daughter, Melinda Mize (center). Melinda, who was on duty with the National Guard, surprised her father on the final day by driving all night to see him take off. Mize finished in 12th place.

CHOPPY WATER - Kentucky Lake has long been known for its ability to get rough with waves caused by wind and big boats. It was no different for the Bluegrass Brawl as evidenced by Kevin Wirth's trolling motor bouncing completely out of the water on Day Three. Wirth finished in 2nd place in the event.

5th Place
John Crews

4th Place
Skeet Reese

Pos.	Name	Hometown	Fish	Weight	Money
1.	Morizo Shimizu	Murrieta, Calif.	20	66-09	$103,000.00
2.	Kevin Wirth	Crestwood, Ky.	20	64-14	$30,000.00
3.	Kevin VanDam	Kalamazoo, Mich.	20	63-08	$26,000.00

Pos.	Name	Hometown	Fish	Weight	Money
4.	Skeet Reese	Auburn, Calif.	20	61-11	$18,000.00
5.	John Crews	Salem, Va.	20	61-01	$17,000.00
6.	Jeff Kriet	Ardmore, Okla.	20	60-08	$15,500.00

3rd Place
Kevin VanDam

2nd Place
Kevin Wirth

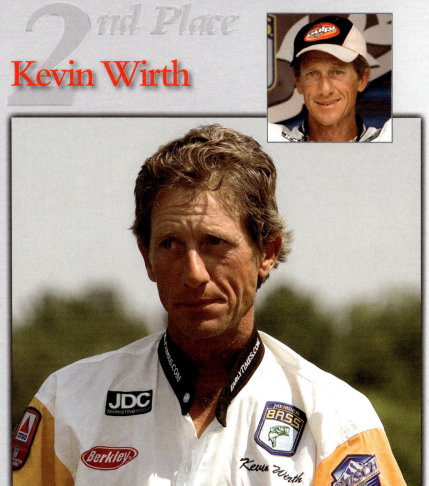

Pos.	Name	Hometown	Fish	Weight	Money	Pos.	Name	Hometown	Fish	Weight	Money
7.	Lee Bailey	Boaz, Ala.	20	60-07	$15,000.00	10.	Tommy Biffle	Wagoner, Okla.	18	52-11	$13,500.00
8.	Edwin Evers	Talala, Okla.	20	56-07	$15,500.00	11.	Kelly Jordon	Mineola, Texas	19	52-00	$12,500.00
9.	Mike Wurm	Hot Springs, Ark.	20	55-15	$14,000.00	12.	Jimmy Mize	Ben Lomond, Ark.	17	46-09	$12,300.00

CHAMPION
Morizo Shimizu

Bluegrass Brawl

UNEXPECTED WINNER
Morizo Shimizu reacts (right) after realizing he had won the Bluegrass Brawl. His victory was unexpected, considering he had started the event in 49th place. His last-day 20 pound, 6 ounce stringer gave him the win and forced an emotional outburst (far right) when he hoisted the champion's trophy.

JAPANESE DOMINANCE - Morizo Shimizu holds up two of his final-day largemouth bass that helped him win the Bluegrass Brawl.

Morizo Shimizu, a 35-year-old native of Osaka, Japan, overcame driving rains and powerful wind gusts to clinch his first CITGO Bassmaster Elite Series victory at the Bluegrass Brawl on Kentucky Lake with a four-day total of 66 pounds, 9 ounces.

"Unbelievable and awesome," Shimizu said to the crowd shortly after winning the Bluegrass Brawl title. "A dream come true."

Shimizu's victory wasn't expected after Day One when he found himself in 49th place with a weight of 11 pounds, 7 ounces. But he moved from neighboring Lake Barkley to Kentucky Lake on Day Two and caught the biggest bag (19-3) that day. He fished solely on Kentucky Lake for the weekend and continued to climb up the leaderboard.

He caught his largest fish at noon on Day Four where the Moors Resort Creek meets Big Bear Creek. He had much of his success earlier in the tournament using crankbaits, but couldn't get the quality bites he was seeking. A switch to a football jig and a Texas-rigged, curly-tailed, 9 1/2-inch Strike King worm on Day Four proved to be key in bagging the largest limit of the event.

FIST PUMP
Morizo Shimizu raises his fist in victory at the Bluegrass Brawl. He overcame driving rains and powerful winds on the final day to weigh in the tournament's heaviest stringer, 20-6, and the day's largest bass, 5-7.

Empire Chase
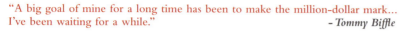 Oneida Lake

"A big goal of mine for a long time has been to make the million-dollar mark... I've been waiting for a while."
— Tommy Biffle

SYRACUSE, N.Y. — It was supposed to be all about the smallmouth. But Tommy Biffle didn't get the memo.

The Oklahoma angler never wavered from the belief that the "greenfish would turn into greenbacks" and that he could win the CITGO Bassmaster Elite Series Empire Chase presented by Mahindra Tractors on Oneida Lake.

Green fish in Biffle's book equates to largemouth bass, a species that history said couldn't win on Oneida. In one of the most competitive Bassmaster tournaments ever, Biffle went against the grain to earn the $100,000 first place prize. Oneida Lake, located near Syracuse, is chock full of smallmouth bass.

Biffle's final five-bass limit of 16 pounds even gave him a four-day total of 63 pounds, 10 ounces. That was 2 pounds, 15 ounces more than second-place finisher Charlie Youngers of Geneva, Fla., who finished with 60-11. And it came in a tournament where ounces were the equivalent of pounds in any other event. Only five ounces separated second place and seventh place in the final standings.

Catching a five-bass limit was no problem for the 102 pro anglers entered in the Empire Chase — 99 limits were weighed-in on Day One, 100 on Day Two, 50 when the field was cut to 50 on Day Three and all 12 finalists had a limit on Day Four. But in an event where only one five-pound bass was caught, the key was finding some bigger fish, even if only slightly bigger. For the anglers focusing on smallmouth bass, that meant culling through dozens and dozens of two- to two-and-a-half-pounders per day.

"This is probably the most fun tournament I've ever fished that I didn't win," said Kevin VanDam, who took third place with a total of 60 pounds, 8 ounces.

Basstracker, a method used to track the anglers' catch on the last day of the tournament when all 12 have TV cameras recording their every move, showed that VanDam caught over 100 pounds of smallmouth bass Sunday.

Almost every angler targeting smallmouths complained of skinned and bleeding fingers from the multiple abrasions endured in taking fish off the hook to release them.

"The only regret I have is that I didn't get to catch 100 fish a day," said Biffle.

"These are the worst types of tournaments from a strategy standpoint. I know what to do if I'm behind somewhere else and have to catch up. I can gamble to catch 20 pounds. Here, it's like a horse race. You can't make up ground. The first one out of the gate wins, the horse that stumbles, loses. There ain't no catching up."

– Gerald Swindle

THE LARGE AND SMALL OF IT - The CITGO Bassmaster Elite Series Empire Chase presented by Mahindra Tractors was slated as a smallmouth tournament. There were plenty of the brown fish caught, but this event quickly became all about largemouth. Lee Bailey (left) set the tone on Day One taking the lead with more than 18 pounds, and Tommy Biffle (far left) spent his time in ultra-shallow water (above) to win the event with four straight days of nothing but largemouth that totaled 63 pounds, 10 ounces.

BIGGIE SMALLMOUTH - Michael Iaconelli (above) holds up a smallmouth caught from Oneida Lake. While smallmouth didn't win the event, they did account for several top finishes. Iaconelli, who is considered a smallmouth expert, finished in 6th place in the event.

NEW YORK FANS - Bass fishing may be centered in the Southeast, but bass fans in New York showed just how rabid they could be. They included three young fans (left) who showed their support of Kevin VanDam by painting his initials on their chests. And a young fan (right) left little doubt where his allegiance centered by holding a New York license plate with the words "BASSFISH." And if that weren't enough, yet another young fan (opposite page) insisted on gathering autographs on either side of his Mohawk haircut.

COOKING IT UP – Ken Cook idles past the checkout dock during the CITGO Bassmaster Elite Series Empire Chase presented by Mahindra Tractors. Cook finished the event in 4th place.

4th Place
Ken Cook

4th Place
Dave Wolak

Tie

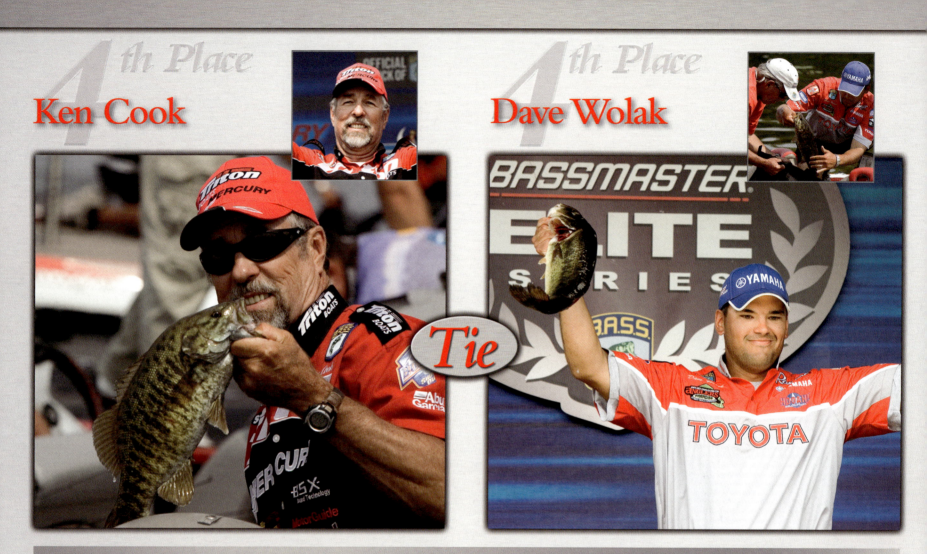

Pos.	Name	Hometown	Fish	Weight	Money
1.	Tommy Biffle	Wagoner, Okla.	20	63-10	$101,500.00
2.	Charlie Youngers	Geneva, Fla.	20	60-11	$30,000.00
3.	Kevin VanDam	Kalamazoo, Mich.	20	60-08	$25,000.00

	Pos.	Name	Hometown	Fish	Weight	Money
Tie	4.	Dave Wolak	Warrior Run, Pa.	20	60-07	$18,500.00
	4.	Ken Cook	Lawton, Okla.	20	60-07	$17,500.00
Tie	6.	Lee Bailey	Boaz, Ala.	20	60-06	$17,250.00

3rd Place
Kevin VanDam

2nd Place
Charlie Youngers

Pos.	Name	Hometown	Fish	Weight	Money
Tie 6.	Michael Iaconelli	Runnemde, N.J.	20	60-06	$15,250.00
8.	Bernie Schultz	Gainsville, Fla.	20	59-03	$14,500.00
9.	Yusuke Miyazaki	Mineola, Texas	20	58-10	$14,000.00

Pos.	Name	Hometown	Fish	Weight	Money
10.	Timmy Horton	Muscle Shoals, Ala.	20	58-08	$13,500.00
11.	Matt Reed	Madisonville, Texas	20	57-06	$13,500.00
12.	Russ Lane	Prattville, Ala.	20	55-10	$12,300.00

Tommy Biffle

Empire Chase

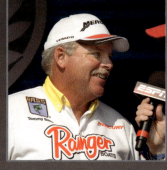

MILLIONAIRE - Tommy Biffle's victory at the Empire Chase was even more convincing considering he won the event with an almost three-pound cushion over Charlie Youngers. That came in an event where ounces were the equivalent of pounds in any other event. Only five ounces separated second place and seventh place in the final standings.

Tommy Biffle's hardheaded approach was the perfect recipe for winning the CITGO Bassmaster Elite Series Empire Chase presented by Mahindra Tractors on Oneida Lake.

Tournament history on this lake indicated you couldn't win by targeting only largemouth bass. But Biffle never wavered in his belief that the "green fish would turn into greenbacks."

Biffle's final five-bass limit of 16 pounds even gave him a four-day winning total of 63 pounds, 10 ounces. And the $100,000 paycheck made him only the 16th professional angler to reach the milestone of $1 million in Bassmaster earnings.

"A big goal of mine for a long time has been to make the million-dollar mark in BASS," Biffle said. "I've been waiting for awhile."

Biffle's key to success was very shallow, shaded water — often near undercut banks. His primary lure was a Reaction Innovations Sweet Beaver soft plastic in a green pumpkin/watermelon color pattern combination.

The lure was weighted with a quarter-ounce Tru-Tungsten slip-sinker in a color pattern that matched the soft plastic.

He was flipping that lure into as little as six-inches of clear water.

"That's kind of hard to do when you can see every pebble on the bottom," said Biffle, who said he'd occasionally flip the lure on dry ground before reeling it into the water.

Biffle's other lure of choice was a Ribbit Frog, also fished in very shallow water.

"I'm kind of proud of myself," Biffle said after the win. "I made a lot of good decisions."

SHALLOW CHAMP - Tommy Biffle never wavered from his belief that the Empire Chase could be won on largemouth bass. Despite warnings that the shallow-water fish would eventually run out, Biffle stayed shallow (left), oftentimes casting in water where he could see every pebble. His confidence in his choice proved the difference in allowing him to win his first Bassmaster event since 1995.

FULL PRESS - An army of press gathers around Tommy Biffle moments after he won the Empire Chase on Oneida Lake.

Champion's Choice
Lake Champlain

"Execution-wise, I don't know if it was the best tournament I've ever had, but it's close."
— *Denny Brauer*

PLATTSBURGH, N.Y. — From the beginning, the CITGO Bassmaster Elite Series Champion's Choice on Lake Champlain was an unusual tournament.

The lake is known for smallmouth bass. But Champlain was four feet above its normal level, and the largemouth bass moved into shallow water, just like they do on any other lake when the water level rises. And like they do at every other lake, the flippers dominate.

Denny Brauer won the event by flipping thick mats of reeds and various other aquatic vegetation with a 3/4-ounce Strike King Pro Model Denny Brauer jig with a Denny Brauer 3X Chunk soft plastic trailer.

Brauer's perfect execution with his trademark lures quieted an up-start rookie who made a typical rookie mistake. Chris Lane, the rookie from Winter Haven, Fla., led the tournament for its first three days. But Lane found out after Day Three's weigh-in that he wouldn't be allowed to go back to the spot where he'd caught his fish the first three days. It was an agonizing decision for all involved and concerned a misunderstanding over a U.S. Fish & Wildlife Service wildlife sanctuary.

Lane had to fish a spot he'd found in practice, but not touched in the tournament. He caught plenty of fish, but that wasn't nearly enough in this tournament where almost everyone weighed a daily limit.

"I just know in my heart it would have been pretty phenomenal for the sport if it had been Denny and myself as the last ones (on the weigh-in stand) at the end," said Lane. "That would have been an awesome place to be."

"Would I have had enough to beat him? I have no idea. But it would have felt real good to be next to him at the end, whether he beat me or not."

MIRROR IMAGE - Terry Butcher races across Lake Champlain reflecting a mirror image of the Mercury-wrapped Triton on the final day of the CITGO Bassmaster Elite Series Champion's Choice on Lake Champlain.

CHAMPION'S CHOICE - Denny Brauer cradles the Champion's trophy from Lake Champlain. The win was Brauer's 16th career win in Bassmaster events.

"Would I have had enough to beat him? I have no idea. But it would have felt real good to be next to him at the end, whether he beat me or not."

– Chris Lane

BOAT RACE – Mike Wurm (piloting the Advance Auto Parts-wrapped Triton) jumps out to a lead in a boat race with Denny Brauer in the Busch boat. Wurm won the race. But Brauer won the tournament.

SIX WAITING – The six of the final 12 anglers in the CITGO Bassmaster Elite Series Champion's Choice on Lake Champlain stand at the holding tanks prior to the start of the final day's weigh-in.

TOP ROOKIE – Paul Hirosky holds up a pair of large-mouth that helped him land a spot in the final 12. Hirosky finished in 12th place.

MAPPING OUT – Lake Champlain was the largest lake the anglers in the CITGO Bassmaster Elite Series competed on in 2006. The lake is 100 miles long, 14 miles wide and forms a border between New York and Vermont. It's so large that in 1998, Congress briefly declared it one of the Great Lakes. The ensuing uproar forced the designation to be rescinded.

SMALLMOUTH EXPERT – Kevin VanDam turns to give a smile to the ESPN2 cameraman following him in a helicopter as he raced across Lake Champlain. VanDam figured to be in contention to win the Champion's Choice because of the number of smallmouth in the lake. But high water took the smallmouth out of the picture.

5th Place
Tommy Biffle

4th Place
Mark Tyler

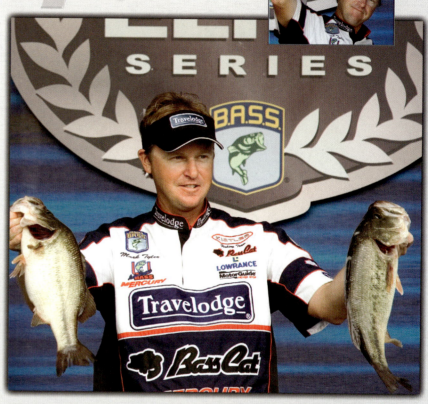

Pos.	Name	Hometown	Fish	Weight	Money
1.	Denny Brauer	Camdenton, Mo.	20	80-03	$102,000.00
2.	Brent Chapman	Lake Quiviera, Kan.	20	72-05	$30,000.00
3.	Terry Butcher	Talala, Okla.	20	70-11	$25,000.00

Pos.	Name	Hometown	Fish	Weight	Money
4.	Mark Tyler	Scottsdale, Ariz.	20	69-06	$18,000.00
5.	Tommy Biffle	Wagoner, Okla.	20	68-13	$17,000.00
6.	Chris Lane	Winter Haven, Fla.	20	68-08	$16,500.00

3rd Place — Terry Butcher

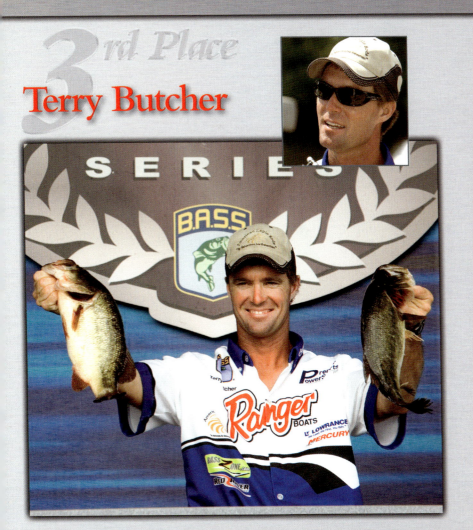

2nd Place — Brent Chapman

Pos.	Name	Hometown	Fish	Weight	Money
7.	Mike Wurm	Hot Springs, Ark.	20	67-08	$17,000.00
8.	Todd Faircloth	Jasper, Texas	20	66-06	$15,500.00
9.	Kevin VanDam	Kalamazoo, Mich.	20	64-14	$14,000.00

Pos.	Name	Hometown	Fish	Weight	Money
10.	Paul Elias	Laurel, Miss.	20	64-03	$15,500.00
11.	Zell Rowland	Montgomery, Texas	20	63-11	$12,500.00
12.	Paul Hirosky	Guys Mills, Pa.	20	59-05	$12,300.00

Denny Brauer

Champion's Choice

16th TROPHY
Denny Brauer's victory on Champlain was his 16th of his career. But he said it was one of the sweetest. "It's not a Classic win, but it's right up there," Brauer said.

When veteran Denny Brauer has "a dream day," you know everyone else is in for a nightmare. Brauer blew the field away with a 23-pound, 4-ounce bag on Day Four and won the $100,000 first-place prize in the CITGO Bassmaster Elite Series Champion's Choice on Lake Champlain with plenty of room to spare.

Brauer finished with a four-day total of 20 bass, weighing a phenomenal 80 pounds, 3 ounces. Brent Chapman of Lake Quiviera, Kan., finished second with 72-5.

"It was a dream day to have on the last day of a tournament," Brauer said. "Execution-wise, I don't know if it was the best tournament I've ever had, but it's close."

Brauer executed with a flipping stick in his hands. The consensus among his fellow pros is that nobody is better than Brauer at that technique. The Camdenton, Mo., native found a thick mat of reeds and various other aquatic vegetation that he was able to mine four-pound fish from day after day. His lure of choice was a 3/4-ounce Strike King Pro Model Denny Brauer jig with a Denny Brauer 3X Chunk soft plastic trailer.

In winning the tournament by catching only largemouth bass, Brauer dispelled a myth about Lake Champlain — that the largemouth bass bite wouldn't hold up for four days here.

FLIPPING - Denny Brauer is known for his prowess with a flipping stick in his hand. He used it and a jig in flooded reeds and thick mats of vegetation to win.

Bassmaster American
~ Lake Wylie ~

"Everything is just surreal at this point." — *Dave Wolak*

CHARLOTTE, N.C. — If you paid attention to the pre-tournament press for the Bassmaster American presented by Advance Auto Parts, this was a tournament Jason Quinn was going to walk away with.

Pre-tournament press and the reality of the best anglers in the world competing against each other never quite hit the same stride. Quinn was a major factor, but it was Dave Wolak who captured the Major. And he did it by beating some of the best anglers in the world at their own game.

That game, in fishing terminology, is "junk fishing." The style of fishing is one in which anglers like Kevin VanDam and Gerald Swindle, a self-described "King of Junk," excel. Loosely, it means throwing everything but the kitchen sink at every type of cover, including the kitchen sink if there's one in front of you.

"This lake fits my style," said Wolak. "I put 10 rods on the deck and cast whatever is appropriate."

With each angler limited to 70 minutes in each of six mid-lake sections of Lake Wylie, it was the perfect scenario to take care of the variety of structure and cover options. And within them the fish had their own variations.

"It's like there are two subspecies of (largemouth) bass in this lake," said Kevin VanDam. "One of them feeds on shad and then goes out to deep structure. The other one stays shallow all year long and really keys on the bream beds. They hunt them in packs, like a wolf pack."

Wolak capitalized on both, starting the event in first place on Day One, surviving a poor Day Two to make the 12-man cut in 11th place. With the weights cut to zero, Wolak led the final two days to earn the $250,000 first-place prize.

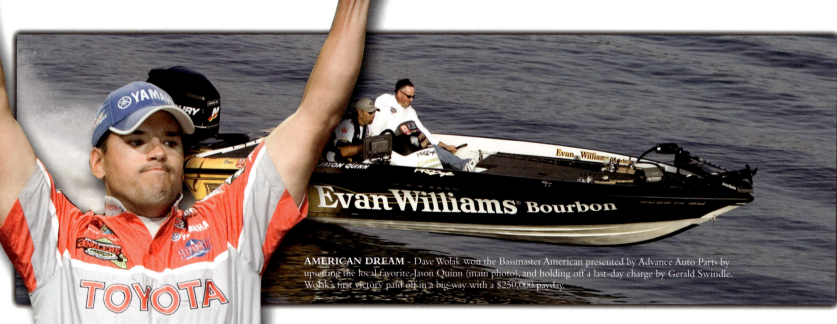

AMERICAN DREAM - Dave Wolak won the Bassmaster American presented by Advance Auto Parts by upsetting the local favorite, Jason Quinn (main photo), and holding off a last-day charge by Gerald Swindle. Wolak's first victory paid off in a big way with a $250,000 payday.

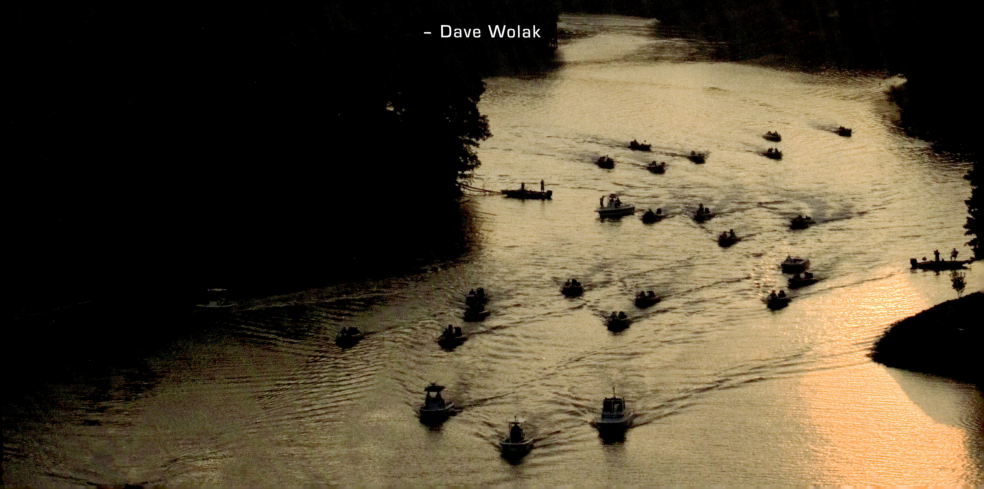

"I had a good year last year, but everything was still tough. I had no sponsors at all that first year. We put everything on the line for me to fish. This will change my whole life, there's no doubt about it. This will change my wife's life. This will change my kid's life."

– Dave Wolak

WHAT'S UP DOCK – Every day of the Bassmaster American saw big crowds show up for the take off each morning. It was an easy way to get close to the professional anglers as they prepared their tackle for Lake Wylie.

LOCAL FAVORITE & WBT CHAMP - Jason Quinn (above) was by far the favorite in this event. The professional angler lives on Lake Wylie and started his career as a guide there. His knowledge of the lake helped him slip into the semi-final 12 and the final six, but ultimately a big start by Dave Wolak was too much to overcome.

Lisa Stenard (right) of Clarksville, Tenn., lifts her arms in victory after she won the Mercury Women's Bassmaster Tour Presented by Triton Boats event on Lake Norman. The WBT was held in conjunction with the Bassmaster American.

AMERICAN TAKE OFF
The final six competitors leave the dock on Sunday morning (above) of the Bassmaster American on Lake Wylie. The event started with 55 anglers. After Day Two, the field was cut to 12 anglers and they competed on a six-hole course that consisted of much of the main lake. On Sunday, the field was cut to six anglers and they finished the event in the six-hole course, changing holes every one hour and 10 minutes.

VANDAM ON THE RUN - Kevin VanDam cuts a path across Lake Wylie on the final day of the Bassmaster American. In Major competition, anglers fished out of their own boats, showing off their sponsor wraps to a live television audience on ESPN2.

5th Place
Mark Menendez

4th Place
Jason Quinn

Pos.	Name	Hometown	Fish	Weight	Money
1.	Dave Wolak	Warrior Run, Pa.	10	25-14	$250,000.00
2.	Kevin VanDam	Kalamazoo, Mich.	10	22-15	$35,000.00
3.	Gerald Swindle	Hayden, Ala.	10	22-05	$27,500.00

Pos.	Name	Hometown	Fish	Weight	Money
4.	Jason Quinn	Lake Wylie, S.C.	10	21-13	$21,000.00
5.	Mark Menendez	Paducah, Ky.	10	19-03	$20,000.00
6.	Terry Scroggins	Palatka, Fla.	4	9-11	$17,000.00

3rd Place
Gerald Swindle

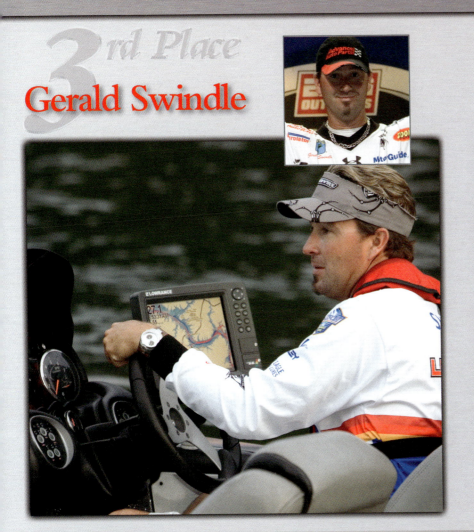

2nd Place
Kevin VanDam

Pos.	Name	Hometown	Fish	Weight	Money
7.	Takahiro Omori	Emory, Texas	4	8-06	$17,500.00
8.	Timmy Horton	Muscle Schoals, Ala.	5	8-02	$17,000.00
9.	Jimmy Mize	Ben Lomond, Ark.	4	7-15	$15,500.00

Pos.	Name	Hometown	Fish	Weight	Money
10.	Kelly Jordon	Mineola, Texas	5	7-14	$15,000.00
11.	Denny Brauer	Camdenton, Mo.	4	7-13	$13,100.00
12.	Lee Bailey	Boaz, Ala.	3	4-13	$13,000.00

RUNNING SHOT - Jason Quinn blasts across Lake Wylie while ESPN2 cameraman, Wes Miller, captures the action. Quinn used his local knowledge of the lake to finish in 4th place.

Dave Wolak
Bassmaster American

QUIET INTENSITY - Dave Wolak is only in his second year on the Bassmaster Tour. He won the 2005 Toyota Rookie of the Year title and earned a berth in the 2006 Bassmaster Majors competition. Described as quiet, yet intense by his competitors, Wolak quietly put together a winning pattern on Lake Wylie to win the $250,000 top prize, just 12 days after the birth of his first child.

Jason Quinn was the pre-tournament favorite, but by the end of the Bassmaster American presented by Advance Auto Parts, Dave Wolak was the sentimental favorite.

Quinn, who lives on Lake Wylie and works as a guide on the lake, finished in 4th place. But Wolak captured the Major just 12 days after his first child, Jake David Wolak, was born and a year after he had won the 2005 Toyota Rookie of the Year title.

"This will change my whole life, there's no doubt about it," said Wolak. "This will change my wife's life. This will change my kid's life."

Wolak's victory was made even more special with how things transpired on Day Four. When he walked across the Cricket Arena stage as the last angler to weigh-in, sitting on the "hot seat" was Wolak's worst nightmare — Kevin VanDam. Wolak knew VanDam had caught enough fish on Day Four to move into first place among the other five finalists. And Wolak knew VanDam's history for winning tournaments.

In the end, not even VanDam could overcome the lead Wolak established on Day Three. Wolak's final-day 10 pounds, 8 ounces, gave him a total of 25-14. VanDam, who has won over $2 million on the BASS tour, including two Bassmaster Classics, caught the biggest bag in the final — 13 pounds, 13 ounces — but it left him almost three pounds back at 22-15.

"Everything is just surreal at this point," said Wolak.

BIG START - Dave Wolak (above) holds up two fish from his 15 pound, 6 ounce stringer caught on Day Three. The stringer gave him an almost 5-pound lead over his nearest competitor and enough cushion to allow him to win the Bassmaster American.

CHAMPION'S WAVE - Dave Wolak waves to the ESPN2 helicopter on take off the final day of the Bassmaster American.

Capitol Clash
～ Potomac River ～

"The biggest fish are going to be in the thickest cover. You've got to punch through it and drop it right on their heads."
— *Kelly Jordon*

WALDORF, Md. — The 10th tournament in the Elite Series was billed as the Capitol Clash - it turned into a duel, several of them as a matter of fact.

They were fitting outcomes to a tournament held along one of the nation's most noted rivers, a backdrop for historic battles that date back for at least 230 years.

Kelly Jordon captured the title at the CITGO Bassmaster Elite Series Capitol Clash on the Potomac River. Along the way, he won a couple of battles of his own: He released a fish on Day Two that would have given him certain victory. That missing fish set up a final-day duel with Skeet Reese that was decided by only seven ounces.

"You've got to swing for the fences," Jordon said. "But it felt like one of those deals in football, where you go by the formula for trying a two-point conversion, you do it by the book, but then you end up getting beat by a point."

The duels didn't stop there.

They were present throughout the event where the battles swung so wildly that no angler led more than one day of the four-day event. Some dropped like the tide, while others started slow and finished with a flourish.

On one side of the win-loss column was Kevin Langill, a rookie who jumped to the lead on the first day with 18 pounds, but dropped to 50th place after weighing in subsequent weights of 4 pounds on the second day and 12 ounces on the third day.

On the other side, was Mike Iaconelli. He came into the event leading the CITGO Bassmaster Angler of the Year race, but lost the lead to Steve Kennedy after the first day when Iaconelli finished the day in 41st place. On the verge of losing the biggest battle of his career, Iaconelli salvaged a poor start with a fourth-place finish.

FOGGY START - A light fog partially covers the final 12 competitors' boats on the final day of the Capitol Clash on the Potomac River. Mike McClelland (below) casts his way to 8th place in the event, while Kelly Jordon (right) pulls in a keeper largemouth entangled in a mass of vegetation on the final day of the event. The catch helped Jordon win the event by 7 ounces over Skeet Reese.

"You've got to swing for the fences, but it felt like one of those deals in football, where you go by the formula for trying a two-point conversion, you do it by the book, but then you end up getting beat by a point."

– Kelly Jordon

MORRIS REFLECTION
Rick Morris takes off during the final day of the Capitol Clash. Morris led the event going into the final day, but finished the event in 5th place.

FIERY LAUNCH
The lights of Tommy Biffle's boat provide a surreal look as he launches on Day Three of the Capitol Clash.

ROOKIE CATCH - Jeremy Starks, a rookie on the Elite Series, had his best tournament of the season, finishing the event in 11th place.

SWINDLE'S FASHION – Gerald Swindle explains to Keith Alan how his day progressed on Day Four of the Capitol Clash. Swindle finished the event in 7th place.

GETTING READY – Kelly Jordon prepares his rods for the final day. The Texas pro concentrated on the thickest areas of vegetation on the Potomac River to win the event.

NANJEMOY CREEK CROWD
Mike McClelland (above) and Skeet Reese (right) shared water in Nanjemoy Creek along with Rick Morris. All of the anglers finished in the final 12, and Reese made a serious run at winning the Capitol Clash. He finished in the runner-up spot, 7 ounces from Kelly Jordon.

5th Place
Rick Morris

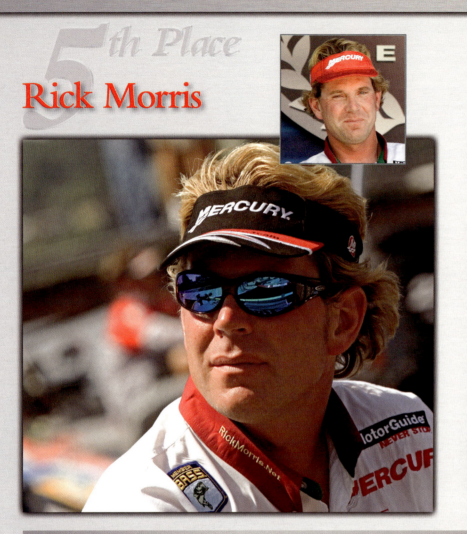

4th Place
Mike Iaconelli

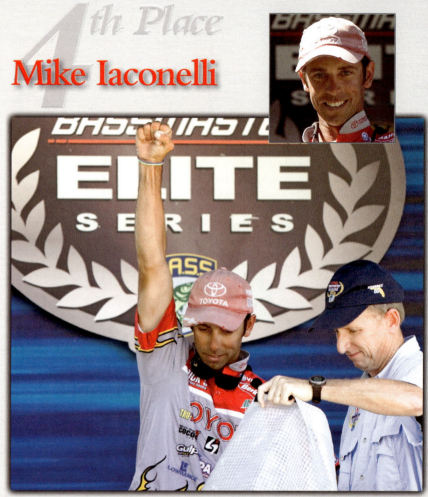

Pos.	Name	Hometown	Fish	Weight	Money
1.	Kelly Jordon	Mineola, Texas	19	60-09	$102,000.00
2.	Skeet Reese	Auburn, Calif.	18	60-02	$30,000.00
3.	Steve Kennedy	Auburn, Ala.	20	57-08	$25,000.00

Pos.	Name	Hometown	Fish	Weight	Money
4.	Michael Iaconelli	Runnemede, N.J.	20	55-06	$18,000.00
5.	Rick Morris	Virginia Beach, Va.	20	54-12	$17,000.00
6.	Kevin Short	Mayflower, Ark.	20	54-11	$16,500.00

3rd Place
Steve Kennedy

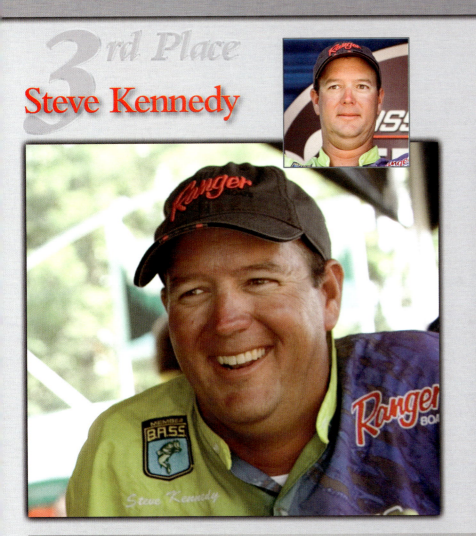

2nd Place
Skeet Reese

Pos.	Name	Hometown	Fish	Weight	Money
7.	Gerald Swindle	Warrior, Ala.	20	54-07	$15,000.00
8.	Mike McClelland	Bella Vista, Ark.	20	52-12	$15,500.00
9.	Stephen Browning	Hot Springs, Ark.	20	52-04	$14,000.00

Pos.	Name	Hometown	Fish	Weight	Money
10.	Brian Snowden	Reeds Spring, Mo.	19	50-13	$14,500.00
11.	Jeremy Starks	Charleston, W.Va.	19	48-01	$12,500.00
12.	Greg Hackney	Gonzales, La.	19	45-09	$12,300.00

Kelly Jordon CHAMPION

Capitol Clash

It was the first Bassmaster tournament Kelly Jordon ever won that he was certain he had lost.

Jordon was backstage when Skeet Reese weighed in 17 pounds, 14 ounces to take over the final-day lead in the CITGO Bassmaster Elite Series Capitol Clash on the Potomac River. That was just enough to give Jordon a sinking feeling.

"You might as well have kicked me in the stomach," Jordon said.

A day earlier, Jordon had released a two-pound fish thinking it wouldn't survive and was forced to weigh in only four of his five-fish limit. He was certain the fish would prove to be the difference in winning. But Jordon's limit totaled 17-15, giving him 60 pounds, 9 ounces and edging Reese by seven ounces. Jordon used a buzzbait early and then switched to a flipping stick loaded with 65-pound-test braided line, a 1 1/2-ounce jig with a Kicker Craw soft plastic trailer to stay in contention from the start, shifting from third place on Day One, to sixth, and fourth going into the finale. "That's my favorite way to catch bass," said Jordon. "The biggest fish are going to be in the thickest cover. You've got to punch through it and drop it right on their heads."

BACK ON TOP – After a winless season in 2005, Kelly Jordon was back on top of the leaderboard in the 2006 Capitol Clash.

SURVIVING TO WIN - Kelly Jordon's relief was evident when he won the Capitol Clash. Jordon had released a keeper on Day Four, fearing that it would not survive for the weigh-in. He never caught another keeper and the decision ultimately cost him about two pounds. It also left the door open for Skeet Reese (left, top photo) to win the event. After Reese took the lead (left, middle photo), Jordon was sure he had lost. Jordon's final-day stringer, though, was enough to edge Reese by 7 ounces (bottom) and produce an obvious sigh of relief.

QUIET CONFIDENCE - Kelly Jordon admitted to feeling confident all week during the Capitol Clash. That confidence started on Day One when he boated the day's Purolator Big Bass, a 5-12 lunker Jordon said was the largest he had ever caught on the Potomac River. "I figured I had a shot when I caught that fish," he said.

Bassmaster Legends
Arkansas River

"I knew it would be tough, but I didn't think it would be this tough, honestly."
- Scott Rook

LITTLE ROCK, Ark. - Scott Rook officially blew the "Hometown Jinx" theory out of the water during the final round of the Bassmaster Legends presented by Goodyear.

Rook, a Little Rock native, earned a victory in the final Major tournament of the season with his performance on the Arkansas River - a body of water he's fished for most of his life. Rook caught four bass on Day Four for a bag that weighed 7 pounds, 6 ounces and bumped his weekend total to 15-4.

Compared to some of the other fisheries BASS visited in the 2006 season, it was a low total, for sure. But considering the extremely difficult fishing conditions the Elite anglers faced in this tournament, it was more than enough to earn Rook his first victory after nine years on tour.

Rook pocketed $250,000 for the victory.

Several of Rook's competitors didn't enjoy the same good fortune.

Among the group that struggled in the final was Day Three leader Shaw Grigsby, who couldn't muster a keeper bite to close the tournament and fell to fourth place overall with an 11-5 total. Sandwiched in between those two anglers were Greg Hackney, who finished second with a total of 12-5 and Kevin Short who bagged 12-4. Texas pro Gary Klein placed fifth (8-4 overall) and Alabama's Gerald Swindle (5-10) came in sixth.

Both Rook and Grigsby were flipping plastics to grass beds for the majority of the tournament.

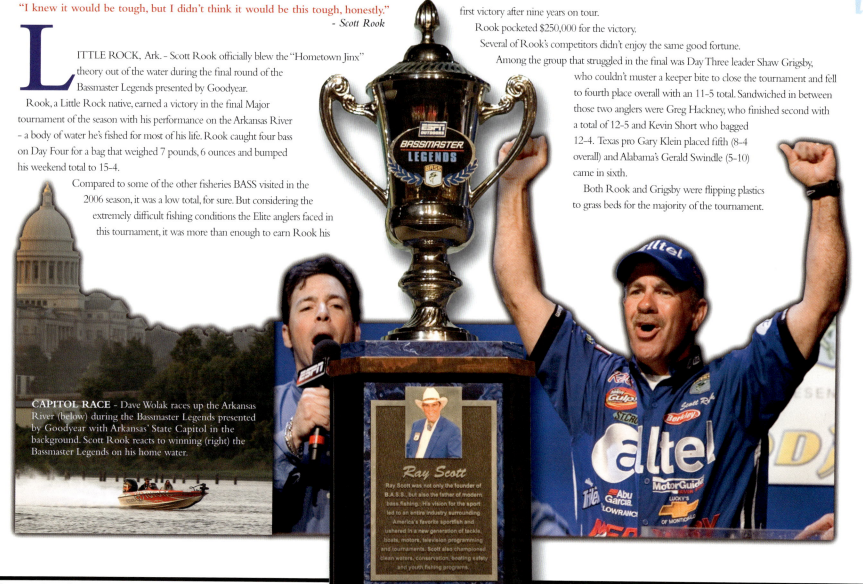

CAPITOL RACE - Dave Wolak races up the Arkansas River (below) during the Bassmaster Legends presented by Goodyear with Arkansas' State Capitol in the background. Scott Rook reacts to winning (right) the Bassmaster Legends on his home water.

"This is unbelievable. I've been second a couple times. I came in second to Kevin VanDam at the Classic in 2001. So I know what that's all about. I've been waiting for this win for a long time. I've fished almost 100 BASS events and I think I've finished every place but first. So let me tell you, I'm stoked right now."

– Scott Rook

BASS LIBRARY - Dean Rojas prepares his tackle on Day One near a bridge in downtown Little Rock that leads to the William Jefferson Clinton Presidential Library.

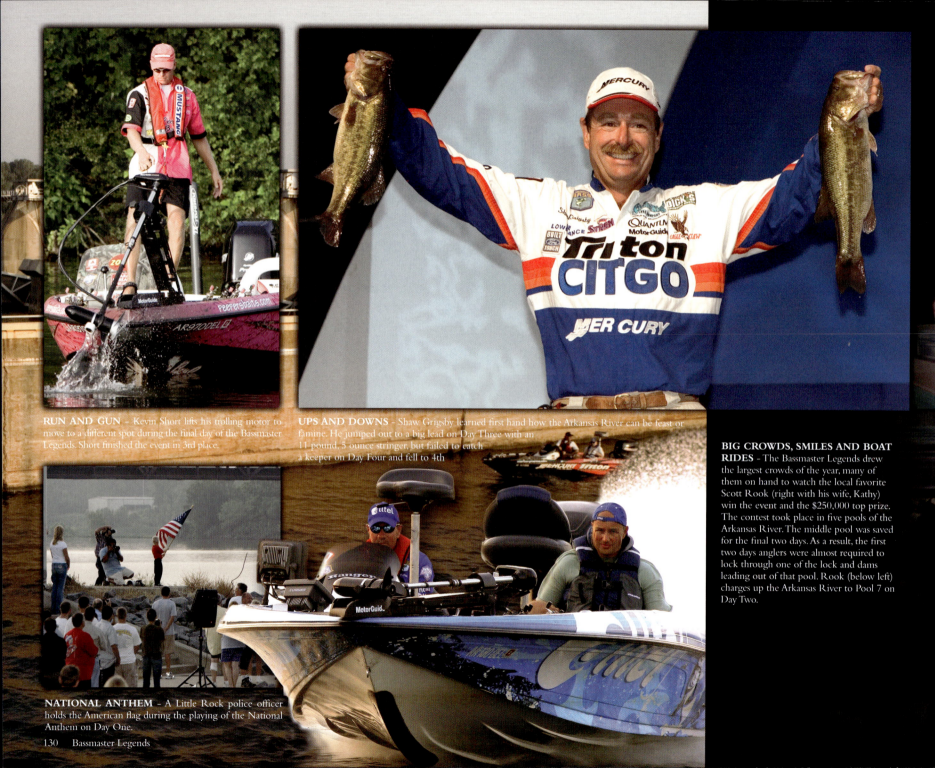

RUN AND GUN - Kevin Short lifts his trolling motor to move to a different spot during the final day of the Bassmaster Legends. Short finished the event in 3rd place.

UPS AND DOWNS - Shaw Grigsby learned first hand how the Arkansas River can be feast or famine. He jumped out to a big lead on Day Three with an 11 pound, 5 ounce stringer, but failed to catch a keeper on Day Four and fell to 4th

BIG CROWDS, SMILES AND BOAT RIDES - The Bassmaster Legends drew the largest crowds of the year, many of them on hand to watch the local favorite Scott Rook (right with his wife, Kathy) win the event and the $250,000 top prize. The contest took place in five pools of the Arkansas River. The middle pool was saved for the final two days. As a result, the first two days anglers were almost required to lock through one of the lock and dams leading out of that pool. Rook (below left) charges up the Arkansas River to Pool 7 on Day Two.

NATIONAL ANTHEM - A Little Rock police officer holds the American flag during the playing of the National Anthem on Day One.

TWO LEGENDS - The Bassmaster Legends recognized Ray Scott, the founder of BASS, for his dedication to building the sport of bass fishing. But he took a moment on Day Four to recognize James "Pooley" Dawson as one of the most important parts of that growth. Dawson was one of the first employees of BASS.

5th Place
Gary Klein

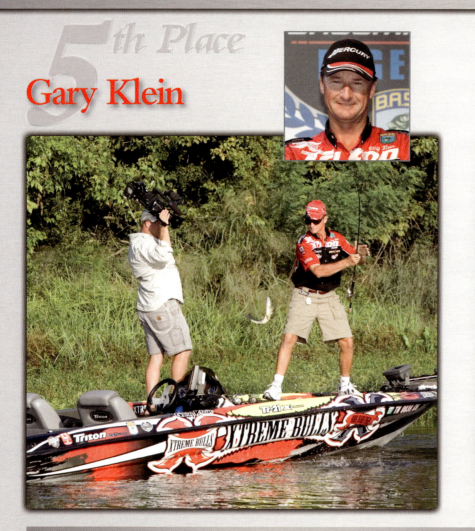

4th Place
Shaw Grigsby, Jr.

Pos.	Name	Hometown	Fish	Weight	Money
1.	Scott Rook	Little Rock, Ark.	7	15-04	$250,000.00
2.	Greg Hackney	Gonzales, La.	6	12-05	$36,500.00
3.	Kevin Short	Mayflower, Ark.	5	12-04	$27,500.00

Pos.	Name	Hometown	Fish	Weight	Money
4.	Shaw Grigsby, Jr.	Gainsville, Fla.	4	11-05	$23,000.00
5.	Gary Klein	Weatherford, Texas	4	8-04	$20,000.00
6.	Gerald Swindle	Hayden, Ala.	3	5-10	$17,000.00

3rd Place
Kevin Short

2nd Place
Greg Hackney

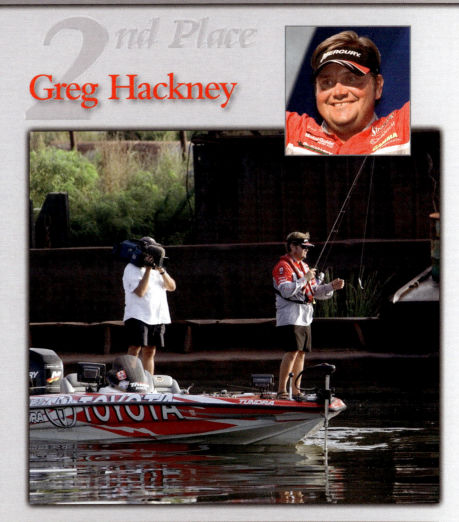

Pos.	Name	Hometown	Fish	Weight	Money
7.	Steve Kennedy	Auburn, Ala.	2	3-06	$16,500.00
8.	Mike McClelland	Bella Vista, Ark.	1	2-04	$16,000.00
9.	Rick Clunn	Ava, Mo.	1	2-03	$15,500.00

Pos.	Name	Hometown	Fish	Weight	Money
10.	Dean Rojas	Lake Havasu, Ariz.	1	2-00	$15,000.00
Tie 11.	Brian Snowden	Reeds Spring, Mo.	0	0-00	$14,050.00
11.	Russ Lane	Prattville, Ala.	0	0-00	$13,050.00

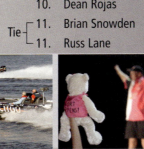

SKYLINE VIEW - The final six anglers in the Bassmaster Legends gather at the Alltel Ramp under the skyline of downtown Little Rock.

CHAMPION
Scott Rook

Bassmaster Legends

The Arkansas River is renowned for its feast or famine production in big tournaments. Scott Rook is renowned for feasting while others go hungry in those events.

It wasn't any different during the Bassmaster Legends presented by Goodyear. Shaw Grigsby took the Day Three lead with a stringer of 11 pounds, 5 ounces, while Rook was relatively way back in second with 7-14. It looked academic going into the final day.

But when Grigsby failed to locate the quality fish that vaulted him into the lead, Rook stepped in. His performance was especially impressive considering the number of anglers who struggled all week with high water temperatures and a lack of moving water.

As was the case for the first three days of the tournament, Rook's bite didn't turn on until approximately 11 a.m. He said his intimate knowledge of the river probably helped him to victory rather than making him second-guess a pattern.

"I knew it would be tough, but I didn't think it would be this tough, honestly," he said. "This week, the fishing was tougher than I've ever seen it on the Arkansas River. It's been hot, there's no current in a month, the water is real clear and there are more shad in the water than I've ever seen. So the fish pull up at night then they suspend during the day."

HOMETOWN JINX - When Scott Rook won the Bassmaster Legends he put to rest a belief that anglers fishing in their hometown were automatically jinxed. Rook's knowledge of the Arkansas River, the toughest venue of the year, helped him put together two strong final days and win the event.

LEGENDS CHAMP - Scott Rook holds up the Bassmaster Legends (above) trophy as fireworks go off in the background. Rook (below) put together a last-day charge to overtake Shaw Grigsby and win the event.

DOUBLE VISION – With the same image playing on the JumboTron, Scott Rook hoists his final day stringer (left) on the final day of the Bassmaster Legends. With the lead in hand, Rook whips up the crowd with a towel moments before Shaw Grigsby weighed in.

The Rock
~ Table Rock Lake ~

"Seven years I've been doing this and I've been close. I just hadn't got it done. But I got it done today."
— Todd Faircloth

KIMBERLING CITY, Mo. — It was a tournament filled with subplots, and the final event in the 2006 CITGO Bassmaster Elite Series had a little bit of everything.

In the middle of competing for the $100,000 and the champion's title of The Rock presented by TheraSeed, this event was the backdrop for the crowning of the CITGO Angler of the Year title, the Toyota Rookie of the Year title, and countless last chances to make the 2007 Bassmaster Classic and the next season's Elite Series.

"There's enough going on within this event to make your head spin," said Steve Kennedy, a contender for both the Angler of the Year and the Rookie of the Year titles. He won the latter, while Michael Iaconelli captured the former, but not before an onslaught of twists and turns.

They included a Day One fog delay, a short fish that Iaconelli brought to the scales on Day Two extending the Angler of the Year race by a day and tough conditions where only two anglers caught limits each day of the event.

"I've been a wreck all week," Kennedy said.

Todd Faircloth, though, held it together and in a manner he would have never dreamed. The Texas pro is used to competing with a flipping stick in hand. But he won this event with a spinning rig and a drop shot, finessing fish in ultra-deep water of Table Rock.

"I would never have dreamed my first victory would have come on a drop shot," he said.

SPOTS ON - Todd Faircloth holds up two spotted bass that helped him win the The Rock on Table Rock Lake. Faircloth won the event by drop shotting, a complete change of pace for an angler known for his power fishing ability.

"When you can go over a fish and see him on your graph and drop the bait down, it's incredible. I don't know how many times I did that this week. You just shake it and they bite. It's like using live bait. He's going to eat it."

– Todd Faircloth

FAMILY AFFAIR - Todd Faircloth poses with his wife, Angie, and son, Hudson. Faircloth's family was on hand on Day Four to wish him good luck at the take off. Faircloth went on to win the event.

TV TIME - Billy Chapman, "Bassmaster Television" producer, directs cameras and on-the-water footage during the weigh-in. At each of the Elite Series events, the weigh-in and footage from the day's action was telecast over a JumboTron for the spectators to watch.

GRIGSBY MISFORTUNE - Shaw Grigsby holds up a big spotted bass on Day Three of The Rock. Grigsby finished in 12th place. The fishing was so tough at the event - Grigsby had assumed that he had failed to make the final 12 cut. During the weigh-in, he had a conversation about catching fish on the lake with a Co-Angler. When he later learned he had made the cut, he realized the conversation was against BASS's no-information rule and had to withdraw from the final day.

VARIETY OF THE ROCK - The storylines were countless at The Rock. They started with a Day One fog delay. Trip Weldon (lower left) waits at the end of the dock while the Missouri Water Patrol returns with a report on how soon the fog might lift. The delay lasted 1 hour, 45 minutes. And it wasn't only fog; on Day Three it started raining and continued throughout the weigh-in (upper left). All the changes created drama centering around the CITGO Angler of the Year race. Michael Iaconelli (lower right) held on to win the title. The tournament itself had its own twists and turns. Part of the final day field concentrated on shallow water up one of the main tributaries like Skeet Reese (big photo) who ran way up the James River to finish in 10th place. The other half of the field were perched on the bows of their boats intently watching their electronics, like Edwin Evers (above) catching suspended fish down to 30-feet or deeper. Evers finished in 2nd place in the event.

5th Place — Jon Bondy

4th Place — Bill Lowen

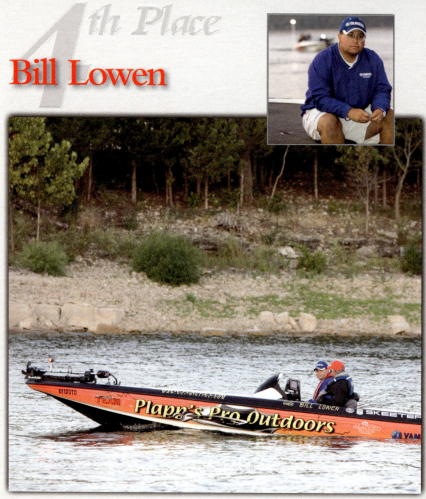

Pos.	Name	Hometown	Fish	Weight	Money
1.	Todd Faircloth	Jasper, Texas	20	50-09	$101,000.00
2.	Edwin Evers	Talala, Okla.	20	46-03	$30,000.00
3.	Kevin Short	Mayflower, Ark.	18	45-14	$25,000.00

Pos.	Name	Hometown	Fish	Weight	Money
4.	Bill Lowen	North Bend, Ohio	17	43-13	$19,000.00
5.	Jon Bondy	Windsor, Canada	18	42-06	$17,000.00
6.	William Smith, Jr.	Somerset, Ky.	18	41-00	$15,500.00

3rd Place
Kevin Short

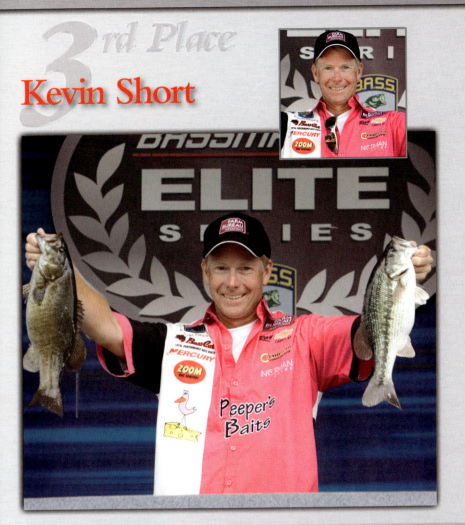

2nd Place
Edwin Evers

Pos.	Name	Hometown	Fish	Weight	Money
7.	Ishama Monroe	Hughson, Calif.	14	36-08	$15,500.00
8.	Tommy Biffle	Wagoner, Okla.	15	36-00	$14,500.00
9.	Brian Snowden	Reeds Spring, Mo.	17	35-11	$14,000.00

Pos.	Name	Hometown	Fish	Weight	Money
10.	Skeet Reese	Auburn, Calif.	12	34-09	$15,500.00
11.	John Murray	Phoenix, Ariz.	12	32-10	$13,500.00
12.	Shaw Grigsby, Jr.	Gainesville, Fla.	11	27-08	$12,300.00

Todd Faircloth

CHAMPION

The Rock

The last time Todd Faircloth fished on Table Rock Lake, he didn't fare well and lost a berth in the CITGO Bassmaster Classic.

This time around, Faircloth earned some redemption.

Faircloth, who hails from Jasper, Texas, won The Rock presented by TheraSeed — the final tournament of the 2006 CITGO Bassmaster Elite Series. His four-day total of 50 pounds, 9 ounces, propelled him to the victory, earned him a $100,000 check and secured him a spot in the 2007 Bassmaster Classic.

It was Faircloth's first victory in his seven years as a professional angler.

"I'm emotional," Faircloth said, as he choked back tears. "It's all coming out. Where to start? Seven years I've been doing this and I've been close. I just hadn't got it done. But I got it done today."

Faircloth was fishing in approximately 30 to 35 feet of water at the James River near Indian Point south of Table Rock Lake.

He used a drop-shot rigged with a 5-inch Senko Slim Worm (green pumpkin color) to land all of his bass on the final day — the same lure that made him one of only two anglers who caught a limit of fish each day of the tournament.

He looked for underwater contour near deep drop-offs and specifically targeted gravel flats to land his biggest fish.

DETERMINED - Todd Faircloth has been winless as a Bassmaster professional in seven years. But he changed that at The Rock in an uncharacteristic fashion. Faircloth is known for his prowess with a flipping stick in his hand, but at The Rock he won the event by finessing deep-water spotted bass with a spinning reel. The Texas pro had practiced the technique on Sam Rayburn Reservoir to prepare for the final event. At the time he was more worried about losing a berth in the Bassmaster Classic than winning, saying he would have never dreamed he would win his first event with a spinning rod and reel in his hands.

EMOTION AND PRIDE - Todd Faircloth (top photo) wipes a tear from his eyes after receiving the champion's trophy at The Rock. Faircloth, known for his quiet, steadfast approach to fishing, became emotional while telling the weigh-in crowd how long he had waited for that moment. Faircloth covers his heart (bottom photo) during the playing of the National Anthem, the traditional precursor to the take-off on the final day.

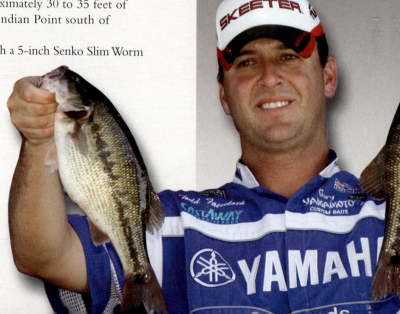

Mike Iaconelli
ANGLER of the YEAR

After a 24-hour nightmare, Mike Iaconelli finally experienced a dream come true. The 34-year-old Runnemede, N.J. native left the door open on Day Two for the CITGO Bassmaster Elite Series Angler of the Year title. But he recovered to shut that door and earn the $125,000 bonus that goes with it on Day Three at Table Rock Lake.

"I've been dreaming about this since I was 13 years old," Iaconelli said. "It's amazing."

Maybe even more impressive was the pressure Iaconelli survived from the Day Three weigh-in until the title was secured. Iaconelli suffered a penalty for weighing-in a bass just under the 15-inch minimum. It left him in 48th place at The Rock presented by TheraSeed. He made the top-50, two-day cut by a mere 4 ounces.

Plus he had three-time BASS Angler of the Year Kevin Van-Dam and Toyota Rookie of the Year Steve Kennedy hot on his heels. Red hot, in fact, because of Iaconelli's mistake.

"I've never, never in forever had a hard time sleeping before a tournament," Iaconelli said. "I went to bed fine (Friday night). But I woke up at 1:30 (a.m.) and never went back to bed."

Iaconelli at least used his time wisely, after only four hours of sleep.

"A lot of it wasn't nervousness, it wasn't panic," Iaconelli said. "It was going over and over in my mind scenarios. What do I need to do if the wind blows? What do I need to do if it's calm?"

After the Day Three weigh-in, Iaconelli could finally relax. He celebrated with his uncle, Don Fort, who accompanied Iaconelli on the Bassmaster tournament trail.

"Honestly, I'm still sitting here wondering if this is real," Iaconelli said. "It feels great. My uncle came down to the dock (before the official weigh-in). He knew Kevin only had two fish. I told him (Kennedy) only had one. And my uncle just broke down."

Lake Amistad — 68-15

Sam Rayburn — 47-03

Santee Cooper Reservoir — 68-09

Guntersville — 71-13

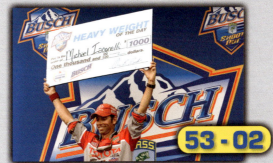
Clarks Hill — 53-02

Grand Lake — 54-15

Kentucky Lake — 32-09

Oneida Lake — 60-06

Lake Champlain — 24-11

Potomac River — 55-06

Table Rock — 15-05

Mike Iaconelli
By the Numbers

Money Won	$382,015.00
Total Points	2,648
Total Weight	552 lbs, 14 ozs
AOY Title	1

IN THE ZONE

2006 CITGO Bassmaster Angler of the Year Mike Iaconelli hooks a big Guntersville bass

Steve Kennedy
ROOKIE of the YEAR

O n one hand it wasn't even close, on another it was so close that Steve Kennedy's dream year came close to becoming the ultimate fantasy.

Kennedy won the Toyota Rookie of the Year title in amazing fashion, more than 350 points ahead of nearest competitor Jared Lintner. The race was so convincing, Kennedy's title was almost a given more than halfway through the season.

What wasn't a given was if he could win the CITGO Bassmaster Angler of the Year title as well. That race was close and wasn't decided until Michael Iaconelli survived a short fish on Day Two of The Rock and the pressure that Kennedy kept on the veteran angler subsided.

"In my first year fishing BASS tournaments, I wasn't sure how I would compete against this level of competition," Kennedy said. "But I feel like I got all the right breaks and cashed in all of my opportunities. The year can definitely be considered a huge success."

Kennedy, 37, started the season in the lead of the Rookie of the Year race by finishing in fifth place at Lake Amistad. He slipped down the ranks at Sam Rayburn, but regained the lead at the Santee Cooper Showdown. From that point, he never relinquished the lead.

Jared Lintner — 2nd Place

Bill Lowen — 3rd Place

Bradley Hallman — 4th Place

William Smith, Jr. — 5th Place

Jeff Connella — 6th Place

Jeremy Starks — 7th Place

Darrin Schwenkbeck — 8th Place

Chris Lane — 9th Place

Jon Bondy — 10th Place

Denny Brauer

HORIZON WINNER

Denny Brauer wasn't particularly proud of the fact that he had a disappointing season in 2005. But he got over the disappointment by the end of the 2006 season.

The veteran angler from Camdenton, Mo., finished the year in 14th in the CITGO Bassmaster Angler of the Year standings, contrasting a 113th place finish in 2005. The extreme turnaround earned him the 2006 Toyota Horizon Award and an extra $10,000 for being the most improved angler.

"In some ways this isn't a title that you want, because it requires that you have to have such a poor year," Brauer said. "But in other ways, it's nice to know that after such a bad year, you can bounce back and compete on a level like this.

"With the year I've had and this award, I have made up for what I consider a down year in 2005."

Brauer, the 1998 CITGO Bassmaster Classic champion, highlighted his 2006 season with nine top-50 cuts in Elite events, earning nearly $200,000. One of those included his win on Lake Champlain at the Champion's Choice.

Brauer joins past Toyota Horizon winners Gary Yamamoto (2005) and Bassmaster Classic champions Davy Hite (2004) and Takahiro Omori (2003).

A WRAP TO REMEMBER - For the 2006 Elite Series season, Mike Reynolds was the official winner of the Hottest Rig Running contest. But the rig produced more warm and fuzzy feelings than hot ones for Reynolds who was officially humbled by the honor.

The experience he had after wrapping his boat in the American flag with insignia of the military and the phrase "These Colors Don't Run," turned a mediocre year in terms of performance into an unforgettable chapter in the human story of his bass fishing career.

"I really had a tough year as far as fishing goes," Reynolds said. "But it's probably been the most fun I've ever had in my life. It's just a never-ending story of veterans, wives, grandpas…they are all talking to me. I thought it was such a small thing. I didn't realize how big a deal it would be. I had no idea it would mean so much, to so many people. I'll pull into a gas station and I'll just get bombarded by people who want to talk to me about my boat."

Reynolds wrapped his boat in the patriotic theme when he found the 2006 season approaching and didn't

HOTTEST RIG

have a commitment from a sponsor that fit his needs. He decided that he would pay tribute to the Armed Services by dipping into his own checking account to have his boat wrapped in red, white and blue. The results have touched many people.

Reynolds said during the season he was constantly being passed on the highway by families in cars that American flags. He was pulled aside at weigh-ins by proud grandfathers who wanted to tell him about the soldier in their family.

When asked why he chose to honor the military with his wrap, Reynolds was succinct.

"They allow me to live my dream. They allow all of us to live in the greatest country…a free country. We can do what we love to do and I wanted to thank them for that."

BASS Crew
THE TEAM

CLOCKWISE FROM TOP LEFT – Chris Bath, Kim Wysocki, Ben Ashby, Cathy Tobin, B.G. Morse, Don Tate, Olugbenga Odesina, Lowell Murphy, Will Sorensen, Sonny Campbell, Paige Green, John Mason, Geoff Carlisle, Gene Johnson, Skip Wilson, Pooley Dawson, Janet Bell, Trip Weldon, Keith Alan, Eric Lopez, Jim Downs, Sarah Cummings

ESPN TV Crew

CLOCKWISE FROM TOP LEFT – Phil Noblitt (3D graphics), Pam Connelly (associate director), Tim Schick (associate producer, editor, cameraman), Howard Downs (Engineer), Steve Dannaway (technical support), Bruce Cash (3D graphics), Mike McKinnis (producer/director), Alvaron Sela (editor), Jerry McKinnis (producer, host), Mark Zona (host), Angie Thompson (associate producer), David Healy (JM sales/marketing), Tommy Sanders (host), Lynne Johnson (travel coordinator), Jake Kelso (editor) and Kevin Witherspoon (2D graphics), Wes Miller (cameraman), Paul Bing (editor), Carey Barrett (cameraman), Steve Bowman (associate producer), Justin Darling (editor, cameraman), Billy Chapman (associate producer, weigh in director), Matt Barnette (editor)

NOT PICTURED - Brian Mason (cameraman), Rick Mason (cameraman), Danny Hampton (sound engineer), Marty Dashiell (producer), James Massey (cameraman), Steve Derstine (cameraman), Greg Goodwin (cameraman), George Small (cameraman), Kyle Carter (editorial), James Overstreet (photo), Robert Galloway (cameraman), Jason Rhodes (cameraman), John McKelvain (cameraman)

For the RECORD

2006 CITGO Bassmaster Angler of the Year standings

Place	Name	State	Points	Place	Name	State	Points
1.	Michael Iaconelli	N.J.	2648	33.	Jeff Kriet	Okla.	2058
2.	Steve Kennedy	Ala.	2591	34.	Rick Clunn	Mo.	2056
3.	Kevin VanDam	Mich.	2582	35.	Takahiro Omori	Texas	2052
4.	Aaron Martens	Ala.	2572	36.	Gary Klein	Texas	2032
5.	Dean Rojas	Ariz.	2493	37.	Ishama Monroe	Calif.	2015
6.	Kevin Wirth	Ky.	2458	38.	Kotaro Kiriyama	Ala.	2012
7.	Skeet Reese	Calif.	2456	39.	Shaw Grigsby, Jr.	Fla.	2007
8.	Edwin Evers	Okla.	2454	40.	Davy Hite	S.C.	1994
9.	Tommy Biffle	Okla.	2420	41.	Brent Chapman	Kan.	1982
10.	Kelly Jordon	Texas	2410	42.	Kenyon Hill	Okla.	1979
11.	Greg Hackney	La.	2404	43.	Dave Wolak	Pa.	1971
12.	Jason Quinn	S.C.	2355	44.	Terry Butcher	Okla.	1961
13.	Gerald Swindle	Ala.	2347	45.	Stephen Browning	Ark.	1959
14.	Denny Brauer	Mo.	2303	46.	Greg Gutierrez	Calif.	1944
15.	Russ Lane	Ala.	2286	47.	Scott Rook	Ark.	1943
16.	Alton Jones	Texas	2269	48.	Morizo Shimizu	Calif.	1924
17.	John Murray	Ariz.	2259	49.	Paul Elias	Miss.	1917
18.	Jared Lintner	Calif.	2240	50.	Bradley Hallman	Okla.	1889
19.	Peter Thliveros	Fla.	2228	51.	Bernie Schultz	Fla.	1885
20.	John Crews	Va.	2226	51.	William Smith, Jr.	Ky.	1885
21.	Matt Reed	Texas	2198	53.	Chad Brauer	Mo.	1881
22.	Mike McClelland	Ark.	2174	54.	Brian Snowden	Mo.	1861
23.	Todd Faircloth	Texas	2162	55.	Yusuke Miyazaki	Texas	1842
24.	Randy Howell	Ala.	2161	56.	Ray Sedgwick	S.C.	1833
25.	Mike Wurm	Ark.	2156	57.	Jeff Connella	La.	1830
26.	Bill Lowen	Ohio	2134	58.	Jeremy Starks	W.Va.	1812
27.	Jeff Reynolds	Okla.	2114	59.	Jimmy Mize	Ark.	1800
28.	Lee Bailey	Ala.	2097	60.	Darrin Schwenkbeck	Md.	1798
28.	Mark Tucker	Mo.	2097	61.	Chris Lane	Fla.	1768
30.	Timmy Horton	Ala.	2090	62.	Jon Bondy	Canada	1762
31.	Terry Scroggins	Fla.	2068	63.	Marty Stone	N.C.	1753
32.	Zell Rowland	Texas	2063	64.	Mark Tyler	Ariz.	1746

Place	Name	State	Points
65.	Steve Daniel	Fla.	1745
66.	Jami Fralick	S.D.	1725
67.	Kevin Short	Ark.	1713
68.	Mark Menendez	Ky.	1708
69.	Fred Roumbanis	Calif.	1697
70.	Frank Scalish	Ohio	1696
71.	Kevin Langill	N.C.	1694
71.	Keith Phillips	Ala.	1694
73.	Ken Cook	Okla.	1670
74.	Elton Luce, Jr.	Texas	1655
75.	Paul Hirosky	Pa.	1654
76.	Britt Myers	N.C.	1646
77.	Charlie Youngers	Fla.	1642
78.	Preston Clark	Fla.	1637
79.	Mike Reynolds	Calif.	1632
80.	Dave Smith	Okla.	1620
81.	Rick Morris	Va.	1586
82.	Kurt Dove	Va.	1583
83.	Pete Ponds	Miss.	1568
83.	Charlie Hartley	Ohio	1568
85.	Guy Eaker	N.C.	1564
86.	Byron Velvick	Nev.	1554
87.	Jarrett Edwards	Ariz.	1550
88.	Grant Goldbeck	Md.	1534
89.	Bradley Stringer	Texas	1532
90.	David Gliebe	Ky.	1523
91.	Mike O'Shea	Calif.	1518
92.	Vince Hurtado	Calif.	1512
93.	Joe Thomas	Ohio	1473
94.	Charlie Weyer	Calif.	1447
95.	Doc Merkin	Ill.	1446
96.	Terry Segraves	Fla.	1435
97.	Bink Desaro	Idaho	1389
98.	Ken Brodeur	Conn.	1383
99.	Mark Rogers	Fla.	1292
100.	Rick Ash	Pa.	1177
101.	Jimmy Houston	Okla.	1084
102.	Brooks Rogers	Texas	1031
103.	Randy Yarnall	Pa.	1027
104.	Robert Hamilton, Jr.	Miss.	551
105.	Conrad Picou	La.	390
106.	Dustin Wilks	N.C.	151

For the RECORD

2006 CITGO Bassmaster Elite Series Power Index

Place	Name	Total Weight	Average Weight	Power Index
1.	Michael Iaconelli	510 lbs, 9 ozs	42 lbs, 9 ozs	100.00 %
2.	Skeet Reese	496 lbs, 2 ozs	41 lbs, 6 ozs	97.21 %
3.	Stephen Kennedy	489 lbs, 14 ozs	40 lbs, 13 ozs	95.89 %
4.	Aaron Martens	476 lbs, 10 ozs	39 lbs, 12 ozs	93.39 %
5.	Russell Lane	468 lbs, 7 ozs	39 lbs, 1 ozs	91.78 %
6.	Kevin VanDam	459 lbs, 8 ozs	38 lbs, 5 ozs	90.01 %
7.	Kelly Jordon	454 lbs, 3 ozs	37 lbs, 14 ozs	88.99 %
8.	Gerald Swindle	453 lbs, 7 ozs	37 lbs, 13 ozs	88.84 %
9.	Kevin Wirth	445 lbs, 4 ozs	37 lbs, 2 ozs	87.22 %
10.	Dean Rojas	434 lbs, 3 ozs	36 lbs, 3 ozs	85.02 %
11.	Edwin Evers	424 lbs, 10 ozs	35 lbs, 6 ozs	83.11 %
12.	Greg Hackney	423 lbs, 13 ozs	35 lbs, 5 ozs	82.97 %
13.	Tommy Biffle	417 lbs, 11 ozs	34 lbs, 13 ozs	81.79 %
14.	John Crews	410 lbs, 10 ozs	34 lbs, 4 ozs	80.47 %
15.	Jason Quinn	407 lbs, 5 ozs	33 lbs, 15 ozs	79.74 %
16.	Denny Brauer	404 lbs, 11 ozs	33 lbs, 12 ozs	79.30 %
17.	Peter Thliveros	403 lbs, 2 ozs	33 lbs, 10 ozs	79.00 %
18.	Mike Wurm	401 lbs, 8 ozs	33 lbs, 7 ozs	78.56 %
19.	Todd Faircloth	399 lbs, 12 ozs	33 lbs, 5 ozs	78.27 %
20.	Mike McClelland	391 lbs, 2 ozs	32 lbs, 10 ozs	76.65 %
21.	David Wolak	384 lbs, 14 ozs	32 lbs, 1 ozs	75.33 %
22.	John Murray	381 lbs, 6 ozs	31 lbs, 13 ozs	74.74 %
23.	Terry Butcher	378 lbs, 7 ozs	31 lbs, 9 ozs	74.16 %
24.	Lee Bailey	374 lbs, 4 ozs	31 lbs, 3 ozs	73.27 %
25.	Davy Hite	367 lbs, 12 ozs	30 lbs, 10 ozs	71.95 %

Bassmaster Elite Series Power Index ranks an angler by his average weight caught during his last 12 qualifying tournaments in the last two years.

Toyota Rookie of the Year standings

Place	Name	State	Points
1.	Steve Kennedy	Ala.	2591
2.	Jared Lintner	Calif.	2240
3.	Bill Lowen	Ohio	2134
4.	Bradley Hallman	Okla	1889
5.	William Smith, Jr.	Ky.	1885
6.	Jeff Connella	La.	1830
7.	Jeremy Starks	W.Va.	1812
8.	Darrin Schwenkbeck	Md.	1798
9.	Chris Lane	Fla.	1768
10.	Jon Bondy	Canada	1762
11.	Jami Fralick	S.D.	1725
12.	Kevin Langill	N.C.	1694
12.	Keith Phillips	Ala.	1694
14.	Paul Hirosky	Pa.	1654
15.	Britt Myers	N.C.	1646
16.	Kurt Dove	Va.	1583
17.	Vince Hurtado	Calif.	1512
18.	Doc Merkin	Ill.	1446
19.	Ken Brodeur	Conn.	1383
20.	Rick Ash	Pa	1177
21.	Conrad Picou	La.	390

2006 CITGO Bassmaster Elite Series Top Money Winners

Place	Name	Amount	Place	Name	Amount
1.	Michael Iaconelli	$382,015.00	19.	Dean Rojas	$162,465.00
2.	Peter Thliveros	$374,046.00	20.	Gerald Swindle	$159,200.00
3.	Dave Wolak	$342,430.00	21.	Jason Quinn	$148,775.00
4.	Scott Rook	$327,397.00	22.	Kevin Wirth	$139,015.00
5.	Greg Hackney	$269,557.00	23.	Randy Howell	$134,146.00
6.	Kevin VanDam	$241,680.00	24.	Matt Reed	$131,200.00
7.	Steve Kennedy	$239,420.00	25.	Alton Jones	$129,500.00
8.	Tom Biffle	$233,164.00	26.	John Crews	$123,381.00
9.	Kelly Jordon	$227,925.00	27.	Lee Bailey	$123,080.00
10.	Denny Brauer	$220,851.00	28.	Gary klein	$115,964.00
11.	Mike McClelland	$200,900.00	29.	Takahiro Omori	$114,982.50
12.	Todd Faircloth	$184,100.00	30.	Rick Clunn	$114,450.00
13.	Skeet Reese	$178,950.00	31.	Russ Lane	$113,815.00
14.	Edwin Evers	$174,500.00	32.	Mike Wurm	$111,934.00
15.	Aaron Martens	$171,563.00	33.	Terry Scroggins	$107,770.00
16.	Davy Hite	$166,926.00	34.	Preston Clark	$104,395.00
17.	Morizo Shimizu	$164,930.00	35.	Shaw Grigsby, Jr.	$102,350.00
18.	Ishama Monroe	$164,332.50	36.	Brent Chapman	$100,000.00

For the RECORD

2006 Toyota Horizon Award standings

Place	Name	2005 Finish	2006 Standings
1.	Denny Brauer	113	14
2.	Stephen Daniel	147	65
3.	Alton Jones	98	16
4.	Matt Reed	96	21
5.	John Murray	92	17
6.	Ray Sedgwick	123	56
7.	Grant Goldbeck	152	88
8.	Fred Roumbanis	133	69
9.	Yusuke Miyazaki	118	55
10.	Bradley Stringer	151	89
11.	Dean Rojas	67	5
12.	Elton Luce, Jr.	135	74
13.	Peter Thliveros	79	19
14.	Shaw Grigsby, Jr.	95	39
15.	Kelly Jordon	66	10
16.	Bink Desaro	149	97
17.	Randy Howell	74	24
18.	Gary Klein	85	36
19.	Mike McClelland	68	22
20.	Gerald Swindle	53	13

2006 Busch Shootout standings

Place	Name	Body of Water	Day	Weight
1.	Ishama Monroe	Lake Amistad, Texas	3	34-01
2.	Aaron Martens	Santee Cooper Res., S.C.	4	32-10
3.	Mike Wurm	Santee Cooper Res., S.C.	3	32-04
4.	Kevin Wirth	Santee Cooper Res., S.C.	2	31-15
5.	Jimmy Mize	Lake Amistad, Texas	2	31-14
6.	Ken Cook	Lake Amistad, Texas	1	31-10
7.	Fred Roumbanis	Lake Amistad, Texas	4	28-01
8.	Denny Brauer	Lake Champlain, N.Y.	4	23-04
9.	Greg Hackney	Lake Sam Rayburn, Texas	1	22-02
10.	Michael Iaconelli	Lake Guntersville, Ala.	2	22-01

CITGO Bassmaster Classic qualifier	Preston Clark	29-01
BASS Federation Nation Championship	Joe Conway	15-7
CITGO Bassmaster Open Championship	Mike McClelland	17-12

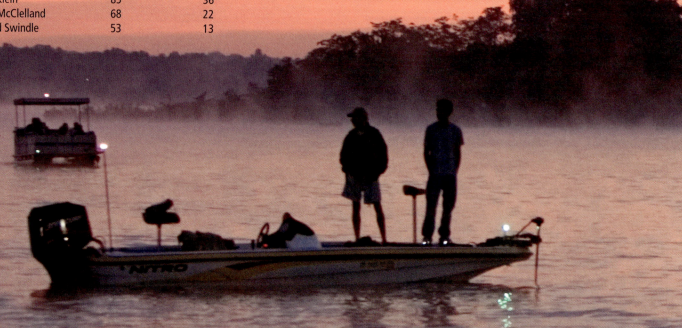

The BUSCH Shootout is a season-long, $216,000 incentive program for pros who compete in the 11-event CITGO Bassmaster Elite Series and three Bassmaster Majors. Anglers with the heaviest bag throughout each of the tournament competition days receive the BUSCH Heavyweight $1,000 bonus, equaling $56,000 throughout the season.

For the RECORD

Elite Series Purolator Big Bass winners

ELITE SERIES

Amistad

Day	Angler	Hometown	Weight
1	Pete Ponds	Madison, Miss.	10-05
2	Gary Klein	Weatherford, Texas	10-05
3	Ishama Monroe	Hughson, Calif.	9-05
4	Ishama Monroe	Hughson, Calif.	9-00

Sam Rayburn

Day	Angler	Hometown	Weight
1	Kelly Jordon	Mineola, Texas	8-03
2	Greg Gutierrez	Red Bluff, Calif.	7-07
3	John Murray	Phoenix, Ariz.	6-11
4	Kelly Jordon	Mineola, Texas	6-12

Santee Cooper Reservoir

Day	Angler	Hometown	Weight
1	Kelly Jordon	Mineola, Texas	9-02
1	Preston Clark	Palatka, Fla.	9-02
2	Conrad Picou	Scott, La.	10-00
3	Mike Wurm	Hot Springs, Ark.	8-13
3	Aaron Martens	Leeds, Ala.	8-13
4	Stephen Kennedy	Auburn, Ala.	7-12

Guntersville
Day	Angler	Hometown	Weight
1	Kelly Jordon	Mineola, Texas	7-01
2	William Smith, Jr.	Somerset, Ky.	6-12
3	Peter Thliveros	Jacksonville, Fla.	6-09
4	Gerald Swindle	Warrior, Ala.	5-08

Clarks Hill
Day	Angler	Hometown	Weight
1	Kurt Dove	Warrenton, Va.	6-11
2	Jeff Connella	Bentley, La.	7-06
3	Randy Howell	Springville, Ala.	6-05
4	Kenyon Hill	Norman, Okla.	6-14

Grand Lake
Day	Angler	Hometown	Weight
1	Timmy Horton	Muscle Shoals, Ala.	7-10
2	Mike McClelland	Bella Vista, Ark.	7-07
3	Mike McClelland	Bella Vista, Ark.	5-06
4	Dean Rojas	Lake Havasu, Ariz.	4-15

Kentucky Lake
Day	Angler	Hometown	Weight
1	Brent Chapman	Lake Quivira, Kan.	6-09
2	Russell Lane	Prattville, Ala.	5-15
3	John Murray	Phoenix, Ariz.	5-04
4	Morizo Shimizu	Murrieta, Calif.	5-07

Oneida Lake
Day	Angler	Hometown	Weight
1	Tommy Biffle	Wagoner, Okla.	4-14
1	Kevin Wirth	Crestwood, Ky.	4-14
2	Terry Butcher	Talala, Okla.	5-14
3	Matt Reed	Madisonville, Texas	4-12
4	Lee Bailey	Boaz, Ala.	4-12

Lake Champlain
Day	Angler	Hometown	Weight
1	Mike Wurm	Hot Springs, Ark.	6-06
2	Todd Faircloth	Jasper, Texas	6-03
3	Paul Elias	Laurel, Miss.	5-01
4	Denny Brauer	Camdenton, Mo.	5-02

Potomac River
Day	Angler	Hometown	Weight
1	Kelly Jordon	Mineola, Texas	5-12
2	Grant Goldbeck	Gaithersburg, Md.	5-15
3	Mike McClelland	Bella Vista, Ark.	5-01
4	Kevin Short	Mayflower, Ark.	5-15

Table Rock
Day	Angler	Hometown	Weight
1	Chad Brauer	Osage Beach, Mo.	2-02
1	Alton Jones	Waco, Texas	2-02
2	Randy Howell	Springville, Ala.	4-14
3	Denny Brauer	Camdenton, Mo.	4-09
3	Ishama Monroe	Hughson, Calif.	4-09
4	Skeet Reese	Auburn, Calif.	4-06

MAJORS

Eagle Mountain Lake & Benbrook Lake
Day	Angler	Hometown	Weight
1	Mark Menendez	Paducah, Ky.	7-01
2	Peter Thliveros	Jacksonville, Fla.	7-00
3	Peter Thliveros	Jacksonville, Fla.	7-05
4	Peter Thliveros	Jacksonville, Fla.	4-09

Lake Wylie
Day	Angler	Hometown	Weight
1	David Wolak	Warrior Run, Pa.	5-07
2	Tommy Biffle	Wagoner, Okla.	5-05
3	Takahiro Omori	Emory, Texas	4-03
4	Kevin VanDam	Kalamazoo, Mich.	4-07

Arkansas River
Day	Angler	Hometown	Weight
1	Alton Jones	Waco, Texas	4-12
2	Greg Hackney	Gonzales, La.	4-08
3	Shaw Grigsby, Jr.	Gainesville, Fla.	3-14
4	Greg Hackney	Gonzales, La.	2-14

For the RECORD

Top finishing Co-Anglers in 2006

Lake Amistad

Angler	Hometown	Weight
1. Allen Ruddick	Las Cruces, N.M.	36-08
2. Gordon Karstedt	Pearland, Texas	36-07
3. Jeff Cloud	Pampa, Texas	36-02
4. Dalton Arnold	Kermit, Texas	35-15
5. David Stewart	Cedar Park, Texas	35-11

Sam Rayburn

Angler	Hometown	Weight
1. Chad Kallina	San Marcos, Texas	28-03
2. Thomas Ferro	Willis, Texas	27-11
3. Russell Lohman	Pineville, La.	26-07
4. Raul Morineau	Mexico City, Mexico	26-03
5. Tommy Swindle	Cleveland, Ala.	25-04

Santee Cooper Reservoir

Angler	Hometown	Weight
1. Tom Frink	Simi Valley, Calif.	34-11
2. Lance Peck	Tulsa, Okla.	33-03
3. Charlie Raia	Gardendale, Ala.	29-07
4. John Proctor	Conway, S.C.	28-13
5. Stephen Williams	Columbus, Miss.	25-15

Guntersville

Angler	Hometown	Weight
1. Hadley Coan	Huntsville, Ala.	30-03
2. Jeff Cloud	Pampa, Texas	26-09
3. Blaine Bucy	Weirton, W.Va.	26-00
4. Steven Williams	Columbus, Miss.	24-15
5. Keith Sykes	Clintwood, Va.	24-11

Clarks Hill

Angler	Hometown	Weight
1. Howard Halcomb	Graniteville, S.C.	24-08
2. Gary Abernethy	Skyland, N.C.	21-11
3. Ed Amos	Dalton, Ga.	21-05
4. Bart Blackburn	North Augusta, S.C.	18-01
5. Jerry Shawver	St. Augustine, Fla.	17-11

Grand Lake

Angler	Hometown	Weight
1. Chris Koester	Winston Salem, N.C.	26-06
2. Tom Frink	Simi Valley, Calif.	26-05
3. Scott Campbell	Springfield, Mo.	25-12
4. Jimmy Sparks	Tuscumbia, Ala.	24-01
5. Joel Clark	Tulsa, Okla.	23-11

Kentucky Lake

Angler	Hometown	Weight
1. Tom Frink	Simi Valley, Calif.	26-14
2. Richard Coldiron	Somerset, Ky.	26-02
3. David Stevens	Eddyville, Ky.	23-10
4. Scott Campbell	Springfield, Mo.	22-07
5. Tom Heintz	Waterloo, Ill.	21-12

Oneida Lake

Angler	Hometown	Weight
1. Donald Bishop	Verona, Pa.	26-10
2. Ian Renfrew	Phoenix, N.Y.	26-02
2. Jesse Herbert	Pennellville, N.Y.	26-02
4. Matthew Martin	Lafayette, N.Y.	25-03
5. Craig Terpening	North Syracuse, N.Y.	24-15

Lake Champlain

Angler	Hometown	Weight
1. Bill Spence	St. Albans, Vt.	31-04
2. Eric Peck	Williamsburg, Mich.	27-14
3. Kevin Cunningham	Farmingdale, N.Y.	27-13
4. Charlie Raia	Gardendale, Ala.	27-11
5. Frederic Jullian	Beziers, France	26-13

Potomac River

Angler	Hometown	Weight
1. Mike Frazier	Orlando, Fla.	22-05
2. Shawn Huwar	Fredericksburg, Va.	20-10
3. Mark Letosky	Warrenton, Va.	20-03
4. Chad Hicks	Rockville, Va.	19-12
5. Mike Acord	Lancaster, Pa.	19-07

Table Rock

Angler	Hometown	Weight
1. Shannon McClelland	Bella Vista, Ark.	20-14
2. Jerry Mcvey	Stewartsville, Mo.	17-01
3. James Hill	Ozark, Ala.	16-08
4. Chris Koester	Winston Salem, N.C.	16-05
5. Art Hines	Joplin, Mo.	13-11

"This is my 16th season, and you go into it thinking it's just another year. But it was not just another year. I think it was a milestone in the sport."

– Trip Weldon
Bassmaster ELITE SERIES Tournament Director